# Blueprint for Life

## Dare To Turn
## God's Dreams for You
## Into Reality

*By*
*Casey Treat*

**HARRISON HOUSE**
Tulsa, Oklahoma

*Blueprint for Life*
ISBN 0-89274-492-8
Copyright © 1989 by
Casey Treat Ministries
P. O. 98800
Seattle, Washington 98198

Published by Harrison House, Inc.
P. O. Box 35035
Tulsa, Oklahoma 74153

Printed in the United States of America.

# Contents

# Introduction

God has given us His Spirit to flow out of our lives as rivers of living water. He is in us to give us power to bless mankind. For years, the church has prayed for "more power" or prayed "the power down," or prayed for "revival to fall," or prayed that "God will move in our midst."

The fact is that God's power is here already, and He — the Holy Spirit — lives in us *now*. He is not going to fall on us, He is going to flow out of us. (John 7:38,39.) God is not holding back His power or revival from His people. We have held back the move of the Spirit; we are the only hindrance to God's move in the earth today.

Paul said in Romans 12:2 that we would accomplish God's perfect will when we are transformed by the renewing of our minds. The mind is a part of our soul. The soul and spirit of man make up the heart, or inner man. (Heb. 4:12.) When man's heart is right, the Spirit of God can flow through his life, and he becomes a blessing to those around him as well as receiving a blessing himself. When our souls are unrenewed or contrary to the Word, we cannot have God's perfect will. His power cannot flow in our lives, and we do not experience all God has for us.

This book is designed to help you become transformed by the renewing of your mind in order to experience God's perfect will in every part of your life. Each chapter will take you one step closer to seeing yourself as God sees you and doing all that He says you can do.

Do not receive these truths as "Bible doctrines" but *receive them as a way of thinking* — although they are Biblical. Proverbs 23:7 says, **For as he thinketh in his heart,** *so is he.* When you begin to think about yourself the way God thinks about you, you will experience God's perfect will.

Casey Treat
Seattle, Washington

# 1
# A Grasshopper Mentality

*...And we were in our own sight as grasshoppers ....*

The Israelites followed Moses out of the bondage of the land of Egypt and saw the signs and wonders of God during their escape. They saw the things God did for them as they traveled toward the land of Canaan. They were excited and inspired by the promises handed down to them as descendants of Abraham. But when they arrived at the point where God was ready for them to move into the Promised Land, they failed. Why? They failed, and eventually all of that generation died in the wilderness, *because they had a grasshopper mentality.*

And Caleb stilled the people before Moses, and said, Let us go up at once, and possess it; for we are well able to overcome it.

But the men that went up with him said, We be not able to go up against the people; for they are stronger than we.

And they brought up an evil report of the land which they had searched unto the children of Israel, saying, The land, through which we have gone to search it, is a land that eateth up the inhabitants thereof; and all the people that we saw in it are men of a great stature.

And there we saw the giants, the sons of Anak, which come of the giants: and we were in

7

our own sight as *grasshoppers,* and so we were in
their sight.

Numbers 13:30-33

In spite of the encouragement of Caleb and
Joshua, and in spite of Moses' exhortation and the
promise of God Himself, all of the adult Israelites
believed those who saw themselves as grasshoppers.
They felt so badly about themselves and had such
doubt that God really loved them enough to give
them the land that they turned their backs on His
promise.

The result was the loss of the Promised Land for
their generation. They spent the next thirty-eight
years wandering around from place to place between
Egypt and Canaan and died in the wilderness. They
saw themselves as worms who did not deserve a land
flowing with milk and honey, and they got what they
thought they deserved — nothing. A grasshopper
mentality will kill you spiritually and can cause you
an earlier physical death.

A grasshopper mentality among today's
Christians results in thoughts such as these:

"It is true that God said we can be blessed with
the blessing of Abraham. It is true that God wants us
to prosper and be in health as our souls prosper. It is
true that Jesus came in order for us to have more
abundant lives. It is true that the Bible said whatever
things we desire we shall have if we believe when we
pray. It is true the Bible says God will give us the
desires of our hearts if we seek Him. It is true that
God is pleased with the prosperity of His servants.

*"But* we cannot have all of those things because we are no good, and God has to humble us."

"God has provided all good things, but we are going to have to suffer in order to earn them. We are going to have to go through many trials and tribulations because we are just grasshoppers. We are just sinners saved by grace. We are just flesh with no good thing in us. When we get to Heaven, it will all be different. *Then* we can rejoice."

The world takes us at our own evaluation. The Israelites said, **We were in our own sight as grasshoppers,** *and so we were in their sight* (Num. 13:33). Why has the world scorned and laughed at the Church? Why has the world said religion is just our "drug," that we are off on a trip? Why has the world said, **"There is no power or anything real in Christianity?"** The world says we are grasshoppers because we see ourselves that way.

How you see yourself determines how you live and what you accomplish. When Christians begin to believe in themselves, to take pride — not in themselves and their own efforts — but in the fact that they are the chosen of God through Jesus, they will not see themselves as grasshoppers. When members of the Church see that they wear the righteousness of Jesus instead of their own filthy rags, then they will begin to live abundant lives. They will make an impact on the world. They will begin to change the way the world sees the followers of Christ.

Jesus gets no glory out of grasshoppers. He wants believers who will let His light shine through them to illumine the darkness of the world. How much light can the world see through a grasshopper?

## The Eye Is the Light of the Body

Scientists say the eye is somewhat like a lens on a camera. The actual sight occurs in the mind. The way we see things is not decided by our eyes but by our minds. The way we look at things, or the way we think, determines whether our lives are light or dark. Light means godliness, goodness, the work of God, or the good things of God. Darkness means evil, destruction, or the devil and his works. How we think decides whether our lives are full of light or full of darkness.

> The light of the body is the eye: if therefore thine eye be single, thy whole body shall be full of light.
>
> But if thine eye be evil, thy whole body shall be full of darkness. If therefore the light that is in thee be darkness, how great is that darkness!
> Matthew 6:22,23
>
> For as he thinketh in his heart, so is he.
> Proverbs 23:7a

God does not decide whether you are cursed or blessed. He laid down the conditions for both states of being a long time ago. (Deut. 27,28; Lev. 26.) The President of the United States does not decide whether you are blessed or cursed. Your family does not decide whether you are blessed or cursed. *You decide.* The way you think, the way you look at things, and the way you see life decides whether you will be under a blessing or under a curse.

The devil already has cast his vote, and he says, "Kill them. Destroy them."

God said, "Bless them. Give them abundant life."

Each Christian has the deciding vote. Are you going to side with the devil or with the Lord?

Do you look at yourself and say, "I deserve to be sick? I deserve to suffer."

Or perhaps you believe this way:

"I am suffering for the Lord. By being poor, or having pain, or being sick or crippled, I will be carrying out God's will for me. God makes us sick to teach us something or to humble us. Besides, healing and miracles are not for today. They passed away with the last apostle. They were just to establish the Church, to prove that it was of God. We do not need signs and wonders today."

On the other hand, you can say this:

"I am blessed. I am going to prosper. I am going to live in health. I am going to serve God with all my faculties. I am going to live a long and healthy life, and I am going to use all that I am and all that I have to spread the Good News to everyone I meet that God has never changed."

You can choose to do one or the other. Those Christians who have chosen to live in lack, sickness, poverty, and suffering do love the Lord. They are born again and on their way to Heaven. God loves them just as much as He loves those who choose to receive His blessings. The difference is that those in the first group have put their faith in negative lifestyles. They see life through negative eyes (attitudes and beliefs). The eye is either the light of the body or the darkness of the body.

I used to have negative attitudes about myself. I was the kind of person who looked at himself and said, "I am so stupid. I am so unworthy. Because I am dumb and insignificant I am nervous around important people."

While I was attending Bible school, a prominent minister at a big convention began to talk to me, and I broke out into a cold sweat. My shirt became a wet, limp rag. My knees knocked, and my stomach turned flips. When he was talking to me, I acted as if my mouth was full of marbles, although I could speak in public fairly well by that time.

Why did I go through that kind of fear? Because I looked at myself as unimportant, as not very good and as insignificant. I saw him as someone very special, wonderful, good, and important. I saw myself as a grasshopper and acted like a grasshopper in his sight.

Later, I changed my way of thinking. I began to "see" with a spiritual, and not natural, eye. I began to see myself as God sees me.

In His family, the Church, no one is more important than another. Each of us, no matter what we are assigned to do on this earth, is equally important and equally loved in God's eyes. He sees each of His children robed in the righteousness of Jesus.

We need to stop putting some people high on a pedestal and others low. We need to believe in ourselves as God believes in us and to think of ourselves as God thinks of us.

Our adversary, the devil, wants us to see lack, inability, weakness, fear, and defeat. That is what he puts in front of each Christian. That is what he tries to feed our minds and to program us with so that we will see ourselves as he sees us and not as God sees us. Who are we going to believe?

> But if our gospel be hid, it is hid to them that are lost:
>
> In whom the god of this world hath blinded the minds of them which believe not, lest the light of the glorious gospel of Christ, who is the image of God, should shine unto them.
>
> 2 Corinthians 4:3,4

Satan wants to blind your mind. He knows that if he succeeds, you will have a negative outlook. You will only see darkness, defeat, inabilities, lack, and failure. As long as he can keep your mind blinded to good things, you will live in darkness.

If the devil can keep you seeing only poverty, how are you going to live? Poorly. If he can keep you looking at failure, what are you going to do? Fail. If he can keep you seeing sickness, what are you going to do? Be sick. That is why one of the hardest places to get healed is in the hospital where everyone around you is sick, and everyone is believing in sickness and talking about being sick. The very atmosphere of a hospital is permeated with sickness.

Even a well person who visits a patient will ask, "How do you feel?"

This focuses your mind on circumstances, not on God's promises or on Jesus as the healer. A hospital patient is surrounded with sickness.

Satan also loves to see Christians in poverty, depressed, or having trouble with basic relationships. He likes to get Christians programmed to watch television, especially soap operas. He can keep them focused on divorce, adultery, lust, envy, strife, alcohol and drugs, trouble, and lies. He can keep their minds blinded to love, victory, faith, joy, forgiveness, and peace. Christians who only see darkness will remain in darkness.

He wants to blind Christians' minds **lest the light of the glorious gospel of Christ, who is the image of God, should shine unto them** (2 Cor. 4:4).

He does not want us to begin to see the good news of who we really are. He does not want us to see what God has made us or what God could do through us. He wants us to stay blind, because when we see the glorious good news, he knows we will stand up and walk all over him. We overcome Satan as soon as we see that we can. He is powerless and toothless. He roars a lot, but Jesus pulled his teeth.

If you do not believe in yourself, you will stay in a fearful, defeated, failure syndrome. The minute the word of God comes into your mind and you begin to see yourself as God sees you, you will rise up in strength. You will not only stop seeing yourself as a grasshopper, but you will stop acting like a grasshopper and be ready to tread on the devil and take the land.

# Identifying the Thief

Jesus came to give us life more abundantly than was ever possible in the world before Him. Everything that has ever happened or will happen to you is explained in John 10:10. If things in your life are stolen from you, the thief was the devil. If things have to do with killing and destroying, they are of the devil. If things in your life are more abundant, they are of the Lord.

> The thief cometh not, but for to steal, and to kill, and to destroy: I am come that they might have life, and that they might have it more abundantly.
>
> **John 10:10**

*The Amplified Bible* translates it this way:

> The thief comes only in order that he may steal and may kill and may destroy. I came that they may have and enjoy life, and have it in abundance — to the full, till it overflows.

The apostle Peter said it still another way:

> Be sober, be vigilant; because your adversary the devil, as a roaring lion, walketh about, seeking whom he may devour.
>
> **1 Peter 5:8**

*The Amplified Bible* translation reads:

> Be well-balanced — temperate, sober-minded; be vigilant and cautious at all times, for that enemy of yours, the devil, roams around like a lion roaring [in fierce hunger], seeking someone to seize upon and devour.

In a parable, Jesus depicted the devil as a thief:

> And these are they by the way side, where
> the word is sown; but when they have heard,
> Satan cometh immediately, and taketh away the
> word that was sown in their hearts.
>
> Mark 4:15

All of those verses show us that the devil is a thief. What is the number one objective behind Satan's thefts? To take away a Christian's self-esteem, his sense of worth or value. The bottom line is that Satan does not want us to believe in ourselves. He does not want us to have faith in ourselves. If he can get you to feel badly about who you are, he does not have to worry about anything else. He knows with that concept he can wipe out your whole life.

To many Christians today, the concept of self-worth is considered "worldly" because they have been reared under teachings or doctrines that include the "grasshopper mentality."

They say, "Bless God, I do not have faith in myself. I am just a no-good worm, a sinner. But I have faith in God."

That sounds good on the surface, but it is a "religious" comment. The truth is that if you have faith in God, then you have faith in yourself. If you do not have faith in yourself, then you really do not have faith in God. His Word says, **Greater is he that is in you, than he that is in the world** (1 John 4:4b). Therefore, if you say you have faith in God (Who is in you) and not in yourself, you are being blinded by the adversary.

The traditions of religion are an attempt to put people down. They keep Christians in bondage by keeping them feeling badly about themselves.

Religious traditions are actually tools of the devil formulated to steal our self-worth, to keep us feeling powerless and like grasshoppers.

## Satan Also Attacked Jesus' Self-Esteem

If you see yourself as insignificant and worthless, every aspect of your life is going to be influenced in a negative way. The devil tried to do the same thing to Jesus.

> And lo a voice from heaven, saying, This is my beloved Son, in whom I am well pleased.
>
> Then was Jesus led up of the Spirit into the wilderness to be tempted of the devil.
>
> And when he had fasted forty days and forty nights, he was afterward an hungered.
>
> And when the tempter came to him, he said, If thou be the Son of God, command that these stones be made bread.
>
> Matthew 3:17; 4:1-3

*"IF, IF, IF you are the Son of God, prove it!"*

What was the devil doing? He was attempting to sow doubt in Jesus' mind about Who He was. The devil wanted Jesus to question what had happened and to wonder. He wanted Jesus to say something like this:

"Am I really the Son of God? I had better do a miracle to make sure."

The devil was coming to steal Jesus' self-esteem, His awareness of Who He was. Satan knew that if he could get Jesus to question Who He was, he could stop His entire mission.

17

As soon as many people are born again, they have the thought, "I wonder if I am really saved?"

The devourer has come to steal and destroy. He is there immediately to steal the Word. He wants to get every Christian to doubt who he is, to question his identity in the Lord, and to wonder if he is really a child of God.

How many times have you done something wrong and then thought, "If I was really born again, I would not have done that. If I really was a Christian, I would not be acting in this way. Maybe I am still lost."

Or perhaps you heard someone preaching or witnessing for the Lord as boldly as a lion, and you thought, "I am so scared and nervous, I must not be a Christian. I must not be saved."

The devil will use anything and anybody to steal your self-esteem.

The Bible says that Jesus was tempted in all points just as we are. Satan tries to steal each Christian's self-esteem just as he tried to destroy Jesus'. His purpose in stealing our sense of self-worth is to make us useless to God, to His Kingdom, and to His people all around us. As long as we feel badly about ourselves, we will not fulfill the call on our lives. We will not live a full Christian life.

We can walk around saying, "I believe in God. All things are possible with God. There is nothing too hard for the Lord."

We can sing all the right songs, say all the right things, and quote all the right verses. But when the time comes to begin believing in ourselves, to put our sense of worth and confidence in ourselves to work for God, many of us begin to sing a different song.

We say, "I am not gifted in that area. And I really do not have time. The Lord has not led me in that direction. That is just spiritual, religious stuff. Let's be careful not to get unbalanced."

Translated, those statements really mean, "I do not think I can handle all that. I am afraid."

Conversely, many Christians look on someone who has confidence in himself as a child of God and who is full of faith as arrogant and proud! We take the subnormal Christian attitude and elevate it to normal. Then we take the normal Christian attitude and make it abnormal.

How do many Christians react to someone who treads on serpents and scorpions and casts out devils, who lays his hands on the sick and walks off believing that person is healed? How do many Christians feel about someone who believes he can have what he says, according to the scriptures? There are Christians today who believe they can do all things through Christ. They believe they can speak to mountains, and those mountains will have to sprout legs and jog out of the way. They believe that if they resist the devil, he has to flee. They believe nothing is impossible with God.

The ordinary response from other Christians around them is, "I think he is too cocky! The Lord is going to have to cut him down to size."

Our thinking and lifestyles have been so infiltrated by Satan that seeing an individual who actually believes and acts on the Word is strange. We label them "wrong," because otherwise, we might have to label ourselves wrong.

Satan has caused us to believe that in order to be spiritual, we must think nothing of ourselves. Most of us have the belief that a spiritual pastor would be one who says:

"I am just a worm. Any good thing that happens is purely of God and has nothing to do with me. I am nothing in God's plan. I just happened to be here when He chose to do something good, but I know that I am just a dog. I am not even sure that I am going to get to Heaven. I am just hoping and praying that I do."

A lot of people would listen to that and say, "That is a good pastor. He gives all the glory to God."

We are to give God all the glory, but at the same time, we are involved in what happens. God's sovereignty is not threatened by our involvement, because in His sovereignty He chose to allow His children to have a part in His work.

There is an old story of a farmer who bought a farm overgrown with bushes and weeds. He worked and worked on the bad conditions of the fields and put his whole life into the farm. He pulled all the weeds, trimmed all the bushes, and plowed all the fields. He worked the ground, fertilized it, and watered it until he had good rich soil. Then he planted rows and rows of corn. Within a few years, he had a beautiful farm with high-yielding land.

Then one day a very "spiritual" man came by and said, "God has certainly built a good farm here for you."

The farmer said, "Yes, but you should have seen it when God had it on His own!"

That is not arrogance. That is reality. God has decided to work through His people on earth. When something good happens, some person had to be involved with God in that happening. God is our source, and we know that all good things come from Him. We understand that *without God* we are nothing. We also understand that *with God* we are everything.

Many Christians do not realize the negative condition in which they live. Depression, worry, loneliness, hostility, bitterness, frustration, doubt, poverty, and sickness are all symptoms of low self-esteem or of self-doubt. If you believe in yourself, you are not going to let all these things have a place in your life. You will not allow those things to influence you. You will rise up, put your foot on the head of the devil, and say, "Stop!"

Why do so many millions of Christians — even those who have heard the Word of faith — live in mediocrity? They know their lives are not good and could be better. They know there is more, so why do they stay the same? Because they are comfortable.

That attitude is like getting in a rut and not having the energy to climb out even if the rut is not the smoothest way to walk. It is like the old chair that needed upholstering thirteen years ago, but you do not want to give it up for three weeks while it is upholstered. It is like a little kid that is attached to a blanket that has been dragged through thirty-five acres of mud and smells like last year's diaper bag. But he does not want to give up the security of "things as they are" long enough for mom to stick the blanket in the washer and come back with a fresh, nice-smelling blanket.

A lot of Christians are in that condition. They know there is more to life, but the devil has them beaten down and feeling so badly about themselves that they are willing to live with what little they have for fear they might even lose it.

# 2
# Walking on the Circumstance

And when Peter was come down out of the
ship, he walked on the water, to go to Jesus.
Matthew 14:29

A person who believes in himself is not going to let anything keep him from receiving God's best. He is going to take risks and do whatever is necessary to receive the best from the Lord.

Many Christians are sitting in churches that are not offering God's best. They know the Word is not being fully taught. They know that the Holy Spirit is not allowed to manifest Himself. But they do not want to leave.

"Our friends all go here, and our families have always gone here. Why, we had all our children dedicated right up there at that altar."

They will not move out of that comfortable security zone and say, "Praise the Lord, I am going to step out on the water."

Peter walked on the water, while the other disciples played it safe. He began to sink — but *he had the testimony*. After it was all over, all the others could do was talk about what Peter had achieved by faith. He actually walked on water for a few steps because he believed in Jesus. You have to believe in Jesus *and* in yourself to be able to climb out of the boat. If you begin to sink, you still have to believe in yourself.

You know that you can reach out, grab Jesus by the hand, and say, "Let's keep on walking, Lord." You have to believe in who you are in Him.

> **Therefore if any man be in Christ, he is a new creature: old things are passed away; behold, all things are become new.**
>
> **2 Corinthians 5:17**

You may say, "I do not think I can overcome this because it runs all through my family," but God says, "All things are new. Old things are passed away. You are a new creature."

Low self-esteem says, "You cannot expect me to be the way the Bible says. I have things in my past that affect the present."

What you are really saying is that you feel badly about yourself, and you are looking for a reason to prove you cannot do the things you know you should do.

When you doubt yourself, you are doubting what God said about you. You are doubting God Who spoke the Word, and you are doubting the Holy Spirit working in you.

*The Amplified Bible* in 1 John 4:4 says:

> **Little children, you are of God — you belong to Him — and have [already] defeated and overcome them [the agents of antichrist], because He Who lives in you is great (mightier) than he who is in the world.**

You can walk up to some Christians and say, "How are you doing today?"

And they will reply, "Under the circumstances, not too good."

But the Bible says that we have overcome the circumstances through Jesus. The Word does not say that we *will* overcome, but that we *have* overcome. You have to decide what you are going to believe — what you think and feel about yourself or what God says about you.

God says we are overcomers, and if you do not believe you are an overcomer, you are saying that God's Word is not true.

I realize that it is easy to say, "I am an overcomer," when you are sitting in church under a corporate anointing. You have to keep on believing when you are looking at a pile of bills or when the creditors and the bank representatives are calling or when the kids ask questions you cannot answer or your husband says, "I am going to leave you."

What do *you* believe during those times when you do not know what to do? Do you believe in yourself and what God says, or do you believe in nervous breakdowns? Do you believe in taking a pill when things get tense? Do you believe in yourself and stand on the truth, God's Word? Or do you go the devil's way by believing circumstances?

Philippians 4:13 says:

> I can do all things through Christ which strengtheneth me.

*The Amplified Bible* translates it this way:

> I have strength for all things in Christ Who empowers me — I am ready for anything and equal to anything through Him Who infuses inner strength into me, [that is, I am self-sufficient in Christ's sufficiency].

It is easy to quote that verse, but do you believe it about yourself?

Some people have been working at jobs they do not like for years and years. They complain when they go to work, and they complain when they get off work. Every time they are with friends, they complain about the boss, about the equipment, about how far they have to drive, about the location, and about the office. Yet, if you were to ask why they do not leave, they would say:

"I am in the union. I have been in it for seventeen years. Just three more years, and I am going to get a pension."

The conditions they are used to, although imperfect and at times unpleasant, are "safer" than reaching out for something better. They have more faith in earthly unions than in heavenly promises. They have more faith in Social Security and government programs than in Luke 6:38 or 3 John 2. They do not really believe in themselves; therefore, they do not believe God is working in them.

There are lots of excuses to avoid stepping out on the Word:

"I have never done it before." Or, "I have not done too badly for the last forty-seven years."

God does not care about the past. He cares about what you are doing now.

Since when did God say, "Go out there and do not do too badly?"

Have faith in yourself because of what God is doing in you. If Satan can keep you doubting yourself, you will never change. You will never grow, and your heart will become hardened.

## Doubt Brings Excuses

When you doubt yourself and feel badly about yourself, the first and usual reaction is to find excuses for yourself. You have to come up with rationalizations for why you do not lose weight, lead a disciplined life, pray daily, or witness for the Lord. The more time you spend excusing yourself, the harder you get. That is why people can sit in churches for fifteen or twenty years where other people are reading the Bible, praising the Lord, and praying in tongues and still remain spiritually dead.

Believe in who you are, and you will be surprised how rich, full, and exciting life will become. Do not make excuses and become a hardened Christian so that you are old at fifty instead of fired up at seventy.

You have to have enough confidence in yourself to say, "Glory to God, I am starting to learn some things. I am ready to live!"

You have to be determined to reach **toward the mark for the prize of the high calling of God** (Phil. 3:14). You have to have a high self-esteem to reach out for the very best in life.

## God's View of You

The first step to achieving true self-esteem, not in the flesh but in the spirit, is to find out how God really views you. Look at the first chapter of Genesis.

> And God said, Let us make man in our image, after our likeness: and let them have dominion over the fish of the sea, and over the fowl of the air, and over the cattle, and over all the earth, and over every creeping thing that creepeth upon the earth.
>
> So God created man in his own image, in the image of God created he him; male and female created he them.
>
> **Genesis 1:26,27**

Both men and women were created in the image of God. We are part of His family. We were created in His likeness, His image. And through Adam, we were to be given dominion over the entire planet. Mankind was to reign and rule over everything on the earth. Satan tricked Adam and Eve into sinning and giving him the dominion. But, praise God, Jesus got it back and returned the authority to His followers, to all who confess Him as Lord and Savior.

Today, through Christ we have dominion over oil. We have dominion over diamonds, emeralds, rubies, and other precious stones. We have dominion over the fish and cattle and birds. We have dominion over crops and over the weather. We have dominion because God created us that way. He did not put man on the earth to suffer through hurricanes or tornadoes or plagues or poverty.

He put us here in His likeness and His image and said, "You have dominion. *You* are in charge."

Psalm 8:3-6 in *The Amplified Bible* says:

> When I view and consider Your heavens, the work of Your fingers, the moon and the stars which You have ordained and established;

What is man, that You are mindful of him, and the son of [earthborn] man, that You care for him?

Yet You have made him but a little lower than God [or heavenly beings], and You have crowned him with glory and honor.

You made him to have dominion over the works of Your hands; You have put all things under his feet.

When we are born again, God crowns us with glory and honor through the redemption of Jesus. Real Christians — those who are truly born again and followers of Jesus — *are* worthy. Not in ourselves, but because of the Greater One in us and because of the righteousness of Jesus. Believing in oneself is a God-given lifestyle. To have self-worth is a God-given quality for Christians.

All human beings have an innate need to be appreciated, to be felt of some value. This need was placed in mankind by God and can only be truly satisfied through Him, through becoming part of His plan. The problem is that all non-Christians — and even many Christians — try to satisfy this desire for self-worth through the flesh, through worldly accomplishments. If you listen to many people who have fame and money, or if you look at their lives, it is easy to see that earthly affairs do not bring a sense of self-worth.

On the other hand, a minister who sets out to build a huge church or a large ministry *that is not part of God's plan for that man*, will not have an inner peace or a sense of self-worth either. His sense of dissatisfaction comes from his spirit man who knows he is out of the will of God. But even the youngest child of God who is willing and obedient in fulfilling the will of God can have a sense of self-worth. In other words, a sense of self-worth comes from knowing who we are in God and of knowing how God sees us.

The desire to be of value, to be appreciated and needed, to be thanked and rewarded, to be honored and blessed is in us because we are created in the image of God. We have a desire to love and be loved, because God has a desire to love and be loved, and He created man in His likeness. Without the desire for a sense of self-worth, for feedback as to whether we are worth loving, human beings would be no more than robots.

When the Word speaks of sanctification or crucifying the flesh, the Holy Spirit is not talking about getting rid of a God-breathed part of our spirits. The Bible is talking about getting rid of the soulish programming that tries to satisfy that need for self-worth through the flesh. For a Christian, looking to the world to satisfy the need for self-worth is "adultery" to the Lord. What we must do is sanctify that desire by seeking to satisfy it in the right way.

Instead of going out into the world and trying to become a rock star who uses sex, drugs, and music to get glory, Christians preach the Good News of Jesus. We are to help and bless other people and to be positive witnesses and influences in this earth. *Then* we can feel good about what we have done. There is nothing wrong with feeling good about what you have done *if it is good in the eyes of God.*

What do little children do when you give them a crayon and a piece of paper? They take them and draw a picture or scribble something, then they run to the first adult they see and say, "Look! See what I did?" They want you to pat them on the back and say, "Wow, you did that? Oh, that is great!"

Now are all little children evil, sick, deceived, tormented and demon-filled? Of course not! They are creations of God. They are good, innocent, and sincere. Then why do they look for appreciation? Because God placed inside them a desire for glory, a desire to know that they are worth something.

When you begin to see yourself and believe in yourself as God does, you are really going to feel good. You are really going to have a good life. You are going to enjoy the highest level of satisfaction that is available for any man or woman.

The world will give you glory if you have nice legs or big enough muscles — but that will not satisfy the inner urge for self-worth. The world will give you glory if you drive the right car, wear the right clothes, have plenty of money, or are in a position to wield earthly power — but that will not, in the long run, satisfy a desire for self-esteem.

## Self-Sufficient With Christ's Sufficiency

Not that we are sufficient of ourselves to think any thing as of ourselves; but our sufficiency is of God.

2 Corinthians 3:5

Because of our relationship with God, we can believe in ourselves. God planned for His children to be like Jesus, and Jesus was not a loser. He was not

31

mediocre. He was the most powerful man ever to walk the earth, and we have been predestined to be like him.

> For whom he did foreknow, he also did predestinate to be conformed to the image of his Son, that he might be the firstborn among many brethren.
>
> Romans 8:29

> Nay, in all these things we are more than conquerors through him that loved us.
>
> Romans 8:37

God knew that you would follow Jesus before it actually happened. He knew you would be born again even before you were born in the natural. He knew you would turn to Him, and He predestinated, preordained, prearranged, and made plans for you to be just like His firstborn, Jesus. He meant for you to be conformed to the image of Christ, and He knew that Jesus would be the firstborn among many family members.

How does God see us? As more than conquerors and just like Jesus. You need to see yourself the way God sees you.

When you face a problem or a dilemma or a negative circumstance, what do you think about yourself?

If you know how God sees you, you can think, "I am more than a conqueror, and this is no problem for me — I can handle this. No sweat."

Your mind may be blank. You may not have the answer or know what you are going to do. But once you make the decision to believe in yourself the way

God believes in you, the answer will come. Your spirit will rise up and say, "I am more than a conqueror," and you can walk right over that mountain as God intended you to do.

> For we are God's [own] handiwork (His workmanship), recreated in Christ Jesus, [born anew] that we may do those good works which God predestined (planned beforehand) for us, (taking paths which He prepared ahead of time) that we should walk in them — living the good life which He prearranged and made ready for us to live.
>
> Ephesians 2:10 AMP

Isn't that great? God planned for us to do good works and to live a good life. He made arrangements for us to win. Whatever God has arranged is going to happen, if we accept it.

God is saying, "You are my workmanship, and I have already planned good works for you. You are going to do good things. You are going to follow paths that I have already set up, and you are going to live a good life."

Of course, He is not going to force us to do good things and to live good lives. He has our paths all planned, but it is our choice whether or not to follow His plan just as it was our choice whether or not to become one of His children by accepting Jesus. Following God's plan necessitates getting into agreement with Him. **Can two walk together, except they be agreed?** (Amos 3:3).

If we keep putting our faith to work in negative ways, such as saying we are no good and will never have anything or do anything right, then we are pulling against God. We are setting our wills against God and His plan, and He will stop working in our lives in order not to overrule our wills and freedom of choice. He will not stop loving us, and we will not stop being His children — but our lives will be unhappy and defeated.

God does not mean for us to have to follow His plans in our own strength, however. He wants to work in us, to create in us the energy, the power, and the desire to will and to work for His good pleasure. He has given us the Holy Spirit to live within us and energize us to do His will.

> [Not in your own strength] for it is God who is all the while effectually at work in you — energizing and creating in you the power and desire — both to will and to work for His good pleasure and satisfaction and delight.
>
> Philippians 2:13 AMP

You may have problems or circumstances that seem too difficult, but you have strength from God. You can be ready for anything and equal to anything with which the devil or the world can come against you. You are of God and have already overcome the spirit of antichrist, because the Holy Spirit within you is greater than anything else in the world.

> Little children, you are of God — you belong to Him — and have [already] defeated and overcome them [the agents of Antichrist], because He Who lives in you is greater (mightier) than he who is in the world.
>
> 1 John 4:4 AMP

> For whatever is born of God is victorious over the world; and this is the victory that conquers the world, even our faith.

Who is it that is victorious over (that con-
quers) the world but he who believes that Jesus is
the Son of God — who adheres to, trusts in and
relies [on that fact]?

1 John 5:4,5 AMP

Look at an example from the Bible of a man
who had no sense of self-worth until he met God. But
when he saw himself as God saw him, he became a
real conqueror. This man named Gideon was called
by God to deliver the Israelites from oppression.
Then he served as a judge in Israel for many years.
We need to learn how to join Gideon's army.

The first step is to decide whether you will continue to live in doubt or whether you will be
determined to run the course which God has set for
you.

# 3
# Being a Mighty Man of Valor

**...The sword of the Lord, and of Gideon.**
**Judges 7:18**

Gideon was an Israelite of the tribe of Manasseh. In his day, the Israelites had fallen away from following God and began worshipping idols. As a result, they had moved from under God's protection and were reduced to hiding from the nomadic Midianites.

> **And the children of Israel did evil in the sight of the Lord: and the Lord delivered them into the hand of Midian seven years.**
>
> **And the hand of Midian prevailed against Israel: and because of the Midianites the children of Israel made them the dens which are in the mountains, and caves, and strong holds.**
>
> **And they encamped against them, and destroyed the increase of the earth, till thou come unto Gaza, and left no sustenance for Israel, neither sheep, nor ox, nor ass.**
>
> **Judges 6:1,2,4**

If you reject God, you cannot receive the help or the provisions of God. You will be out there on your own where the devil can wipe you out. That was the condition of Israel in Gideon's day. It was so bad, they were having to hide in the mountains and in caves like animals. The enemy had prevailed against them over a seven-year period until they were living in utter poverty and in conditions God had never

37

desired or intended for them. They were living far below His plan and far below what is good and right for any people.

The enemy had robbed them and left them with nothing. (Many Christians today are left with nothing because the enemy's weapons of poverty, sickness, disease, and lack of self-worth are destroying their lives.) The whole country was greatly impoverished. Spiritual, mental, physical, and financial poverty had overtaken them.

Then what happened? ... **The children of Israel cried unto the Lord** (Judges 6:6).

When you find yourself in defeat through an attack by one of the enemy's weapons, cry out to God. He will always hear you and will give you help *if you will listen and obey*. But first comes repentance. God told them through a prophet where they had missed Him.

> **That the Lord sent a prophet unto the children of Israel, which said unto them, Thus saith the Lord God of Israel, I brought you up from Egypt, and brought you forth out of the house of bondage;**
>
> **And I delivered you out of the hand of the Egyptians, and out of the hand of all that oppressed you, and drave them out from before you, and gave you their land;**
>
> **And I said unto you, I am the Lord your God; fear not the gods of the Amorites, in whose land ye dwell: but ye have not obeyed my voice.**
>
> **Judges 6:8-10**

But *after they cried unto Him,* God sent an angel with a message to the man He had chosen to deliver Israel.

And there came an angel of the Lord, and
sat under an oak which was in Ophrah, that per-
tained unto Joash the Abiezrite: and his son
Gideon threshed wheat by the winepress, to hide
it from the Midianites.

Judges 6:11

Gideon was afraid of the enemy. He was full of
fear and certainly had a lack of self-worth. And he
was trying to hide the wheat so his family could have
something to eat. In the next verse, however, we find
out how God saw Gideon.

And the angel of the Lord appeared unto
him, and said unto him, The Lord is with thee,
thou mighty man of valour.

Judges 6:12

Thou mighty man of valor! That does not seem
right, does it? Here is a man from one of the poorest
families of Israel and one of the least in his own family, a man who is hiding from the enemy, and who is a
grasshopper in his own sight. Gideon is scared, weak,
under the oppression of the enemy, completely dev-
astated mentally, spiritually, and financially.
Everyone around him is living in dens and caves, and
a faith preacher comes along and says, "The Lord is
with you, you mighty man of valor." Most Christians
today call that kind of preaching "crazy." Yet God
sent an angel to call Gideon *a mighty man of valor*. That
means God actually saw him that way, because God
does not lie nor does He flatter. God saw His plan for
Gideon, and also saw Gideon following it and becoming the way He saw him.

And Gideon said unto him, Oh my Lord, if
the Lord be with us, why then is all this befallen
us? and where be all his miracles which our

fathers told us of, saying, Did not the Lord bring us up from Egypt? but now the Lord hath forsaken us, and delivered us into the hands of the Midianites.

And the Lord looked upon him, and said, Go in this thy might, and thou shalt save Israel from the hand of the Midianites: have not I sent thee?

And he said unto him, Oh my Lord, wherewith shall I save Israel? behold, my family is poor in Manasseh, and I am the least in my father's house.

Judges 6:13-15

Gideon's condition was not much different than the one most of us were in when we turned on the television or radio, or picked up a cassette tape, or opened a book to the message of faith:

"You can do all things through Christ. Whatever things you desire, believe that you receive them, and you shall have them."

We do about the same thing Gideon did — we say, "If, why, where, and but."

If-why-where-but is not a good way to respond to the Lord. Questioning His message is not a good way to talk to Him, but that is what a lot of people have done and are doing. Most of us were living below our rights in Christ, barely getting along in spiritual, mental, and financial poverty. We did not even know we could change our circumstances. We felt so badly about ourselves and assumed we were stuck there. God was trying to teach us something, or this is the way life is supposed to be for Christians, or this was our "fate."

Suddenly we got the message that we could change our worlds and speak to the mountains in our lives. We learned that all things are possible to him who believes. We learned that Jesus is a healer and deliverer as well as a savior. We learned that God will prosper us and even give us the desires of our hearts.

A few of us took the message and ran with it. Most of us, however, began just as Gideon did, by questioning. We wondered, questioned, and staggered around for a little while.

We said, "But what about the things I have been taught in church all my life? What about Sister So-and-So? She was a good Christian, yet she died. I know people who have gotten involved in that faith stuff. They believed it, but it did not work."

We said, "If that message is true, why have we not seen any miracles? If God wants us all healed, why are there so many sick people? If God wants us to prosper, why are so many Christians poor?"

We have the same thoughts Gideon had. When the Lord said, **Go in this thy might**, we felt the same doubts Gideon did when he answered, "How can I save Israel? My family is poor."

The Hebrew word used here for "poor" means "weak, thin, needy, feeble, failing, and dangling." That means Gideon's family was really in bad shape! Gideon felt that his family was a failure, and that as the least of them, he was the biggest failure of all. He *was* poor, weak, needy, afraid of the enemy, and living in a cave. Yet God said he was a mighty man of valor. Who was telling the truth?

In Matthew 6:22,23, we read that the way you look at things decides the way you will live.

> **The light of the body is the eye: if therefore thine eye be single, thy whole body shall be full of light.**
>
> **But if thine eye be evil, thy whole body shall be full of darkness. If therefore the light that is in thee be darkness, how great is that darkness!**

It was a fact that Gideon was poor, feeble, needy, weak, and a failure. It also was a fact that God saw him as a mighty man of valor. Gideon had the choice of seeing himself the way the world saw him (a fact in the natural but a false picture to God), or he could look at himself the way God said he was and move into truth. He could allow the devil to cause him to live out his life falsely, or he could allow God to help him become the true Gideon — *a mighty man of valor.* You and I have the same choice he had.

## Gideon's Choice Is Ours

Each of us can say, "Oh, I am so stupid. I just cannot do it. I do not have what it takes. My faith is so small. I cannot pray very well. I cannot pay my tithes. I am weak and poor and afraid." Or we can say, "I am a mighty man — or woman — of valor. The Lord is with me."

We have the choice to say either one. The sad thing is that most of us have been programmed so strongly by the devil through worldly thinking placed in our minds by religion, television, books, and conversations in our environments that we choose to side with the devil and speak negative things. We choose to accept a false picture of God's children, although in the natural, it may look true.

When the angel said, "You are a mighty man of valor," he was saying, "You are a powerful, fearless champion. You are a strong, forceful, wealthy, virtuous man of courage and bravery."

We need to think and believe that way about ourselves. If God sees us that way, it must not be wrong for us to believe that way about ourselves. Some people may say that attitude is pride or arrogance. No, it is Bible. Real pride and arrogance is to say you are one way when God says you are another. You are exalting yourself and your opinions over God when you do that.

If God says, "You are powerful, fearless, strong, forceful, wealthy, virtuous, and a champion," the humble, submissive, obedient thing to do is say, "Yes, Lord. You are right. You said it, and I believe it."

To say, "No, Lord, I am nothing. I am unworthy," is pride and arrogance. It is resisting and rejecting the very words of God, Who is no respecter of persons. If God said that about Gideon, an Israelite under the old covenant who was not even born again, what does He say about us who are born of His only begotten Son, born of His Spirit and filled with that Spirit, walking by faith in His Kingdom?

> Verily I say unto you, Among them that are born of women there hath not risen a greater than John the Baptist: notwithstanding he that is least in the kingdom of heaven is greater than he.
> Matthew 11:11

What did Jesus say? He said that John the Baptist was greater than any person who had been born on earth up to that point in time. That included Gideon. Then He went on to say, however, that the least of those born again into the Kingdom of God was greater than John the Baptist! God looks on us as mighty men and women. He sees us as champions. He does not see "nothings" and "nobodies." He sees *somebodies*.

How are *you* going to look at yourself? "Oh, I just need enough to get by. That is all I need." Is that what you are going to say? There is no such thing as second place for champions. Champions always win. They are not satisfied with "just getting along." Champions in Christ go for the best. They believe they should do the greatest and go the farthest because God said they were champions.

We need to begin to agree with God, to see ourselves as God sees us, as champions, fearless ones, powerful ones, strong ones, virtuous ones. That is what God says we are. It sounds so strange, so simple. It sounds too good to be true, but it *is* true. If you begin to think of yourself in this way, you will begin to live this way.

Some people think that finding a sack with a million dollars in it or winning a lottery would make them everything they want to be. Some people are just "waiting for their ships to come in" to make them great. But those things would not work to give them any more self-esteem. If a person looks down on himself or feels badly about himself in present conditions, when his "ship comes in," he will sink it. If you feel inadequate and inferior and no good, even if someone gave you a corporation, you would lose it and go bankrupt. You would end up with even more debt than you have now.

How many times have people received an inheritance, and within weeks and months it was gone? How many times has the government built new homes or new apartments, put in grass, shrubs, sidewalks, and made a new city for those living in slums? Within a year, many of those urban renewal blocks are back in the same condition as the old areas. They are just new ghettos. Why? Because changing outward conditions does not change people's inward attitudes or their behavior. It does not matter if you change the outside. What matters is changing the inside. If you change on the inside and begin to stand up and say, "I am a mighty person of valor," it will not be long until the outside will reflect that change.

If a sick person will stand up in faith on the inside, it will not be long before his body will stand up in health on the outside.

A little child kept standing up on the pews in church because he wanted to see, and his mother kept grabbing him and sitting him back down again. Finally she just held him in his seat.

He said, "Mama, I am sitting down on the outside, but I am standing up on the inside."

Children are like that. They will just go for what is in their hearts. Christians need to be childlike in that respect. We need to stand up on the inside and go for what God has placed in our hearts.

We need to say, "I see myself blessed with the best. On the outside, it may look as if I am barely get-

45

ting by. On the outside, I may not be able to walk very well because this body has sickness in it. But on the inside I am prosperous. On the inside, I am jogging to church. And it will not be long until the outside of me matches the inside!"

It is important to begin to walk, look, and present yourself as who you really are. Don't walk around ashamed, slumped over, and self-effacing. Some people sneak into church like a little mouse, hoping no one will notice them. God does not need church mice. He needs Church lions!

Be bold and confident, even if inside you are trembling. Act like a mighty person of valor anyway. Then you will begin to feel like one. You will start thinking like one. You will start acting like one in everything you do. Soon the blessing of God, the provision of God, and all that God says you can have will come into your life.

## Live by Faith, Not Signs

In Judges 6:17, Gideon asked God for a sign. He was not living under the New Covenant where we are told to accept the Word and live by faith. He was living in a culture in which supernatural signs were expected of the demon gods. Also, he was from a heritage that expected God to do signs and wonders to "prove" Who He was just as He had during their ancestors' flight from Egypt.

God took a little offering that Gideon had laid out on a rock, and an angel appeared and caused the offering to be swallowed up with fire out of the rock. Then Gideon said:

**Alas, O Lord God! for because I have seen an angel of the Lord face to face.**

**And the Lord said unto him, Peace be unto thee; fear not: thou shalt not die.**

**Judges 6:22,23**

Many people in the world will not come to a church service because they feel badly about themselves. They do not feel they can face God. They believe if they did, He would kill them. That is what Gideon thought.

He said, "This is really someone from God, and I am going to die."

God said, "Fear not, I just called you a mighty man of valor. You are not going to die."

We need to let the world know that God is not angry. We need to tell the people out in the world that God loves them, that they are important to Him. We need to say that so that they understand what we say. We need to say that until they *hear* it. We need to say it in so many ways and so many different places that they begin to realize that God wants to bless them.

Even after Gideon realized it was really the God of Israel talking to him, he had so little self-confidence and self-esteem that he asked for two more supernatural signs involving a sheepskin, a fleece. The Lord humored him and did as he asked, because He knew Gideon's heart.

We need to realize, of course, that we are not Gideons living under the old covenant. The Holy Spirit lives *in* us. Gideon's "fleece" involved asking for a supernatural sign, not for God to work in circumstances. Many Christians today have the two confused. They ask God to work in circumstances and call it a "fleece." We do not need supernatural signs and should not be looking to the heavens or asking for supernatural signs or outside things to tell us the will of God. We are to look for guidance in our hearts where the Spirit of God dwells. The Spirit of the Lord will bear witness with your spirit. *Do not put a "fleece" out where the devil can influence you.* Gideon got away with it because of the condition of God's people at that time.

The story goes on in the next chapter of Judges.

Then Jerubbaal, who is Gideon, and all the people that were with him, rose up early, and pitched beside the well of Harod: so that the host of the Midianites were on the north side of them, by the hill of Moreh, in the valley.

And the Lord said unto Gideon, The people that are with thee are too many for me to give the Midianites into their hands, lest Israel vaunt themselves against me, saying, Mine own hand hath saved me.

Now therefore go to, proclaim in the ears of the people, saying, Whosoever is fearful and afraid, let him return and depart early from mount Gilead. And there returned of the people twenty and two thousand; and there remained ten thousand.

And the Lord said unto Gideon, The people are yet too many; bring them down unto the water, and I will try them for thee there: and it shall be, that of whom I say unto thee, This shall go with thee, the same shall go with thee; and of whomsoever I say unto thee, This shall not go with thee, the same shall not go.

So he brought down the people unto the water: and the Lord said unto Gideon, Every one that lappeth of the water with his tongue, as a dog lappeth, him shalt thou set by himself; likewise every one that boweth down upon his knees to drink.

And the number of them that lapped, putting their hand to their mouth, were three hundred men: but all the rest of the people bowed down upon their knees to drink water.

And the Lord said unto Gideon, By the three hundred men that lapped will I save you, and deliver the Midianites into thine hand: and let all the other people go every man unto his place.

Judges 7:1-7

Three hundred men against hundreds of thousands! But remember, those three hundred were mighty men of valor.

You may wonder, "How can one church affect the world?"

When that church is full of mighty men and women of valor.

You may ask, "How can we change our city?"

When you begin to believe that you are mighty men and women of valor.

## The Sword of the Lord *and of* Gideon

For the rest of Gideon's story, the writer of the book of Judges relates that one of that small band of men dreamed of a loaf of bread that tumbled into the Midianite camp and overturned a tent. Another of the men interpreted the dream as **the sword of Gideon**

... **for into his hand hath God delivered Midian, and all the host** (Judges 7:14).

After Gideon heard the dream and interpretation, the first thing he did was to worship God. The first thing we should do when God's will is made clear to us also is to worship Him.

Then Gideon divided the three hundred men into three companies in order to surround the enemy camp. Each of Gideon's men had torches with vases or pots over them in one hand and a trumpet in the other. No swords or spears? That is no way to fight — unless that is the way God directs. Then you cannot lose. That little band of Israelites were operating by faith. So Gideon posted his men around the camp of the Midianites, and said:

> **When I blow with a trumpet, I and all that are with me, then blow ye the trumpets also on every side of all the camp, and say, The sword of the Lord, and of Gideon.**
>
> **Judges 7:18**

So they positioned themselves around the enemy camp, and Gideon began to blow the trumpet. At the same time, the men broke the coverings over the torches and sudden flames came bursting out into the night sky. Then all three hundred men began blowing their trumpets and shouting, **The sword of the Lord and of Gideon.**

The thousands of enemy attackers went into a panic and wiped themselves out. They were so frightened that they began to attack one another. Those who did not get killed ran away. The rest of the Israelite army then got bold and strong and defeated the rest of the enemy.

But notice what the men of Gideon shouted: **The sword of the Lord *and* of Gideon.** It was not just the sword of the Lord, but the sword of Gideon. Gideon had to believe in himself before God could set the oppressed nation free. Christians are going to have to believe that they are children of God, mighty men and women of valor, before the world can be set free from the bondage and oppression of the devil.

When we begin to believe that and let our lights shine out and shout about it, the world can be set free. The enemy can be chased out. The devil will then be trampled underfoot, and all those who choose freedom can be delivered. But this will happen only if the Church begins to believe in itself and when Christians begin to see themselves as God sees them.

When Christians begin to believe they are sons and daughters of God, not unworthy worms, the victories will manifest. We have to be unafraid to proclaim *the sword of the Lord and of the Church.* We have to be unafraid to blow our own horns. The devil is not going to blow our horns, and God is not going to blow them. He has placed a horn in each of our hands and said, "Blow."

## God Needs *You*

God needs each one of His children to be active and working on earth. But you have to believe in yourself as a child of God before He can use you. Otherwise, you will be like those Israelites who were sent home before the battle. You will sit on the sidelines while a few brave Christians who know who they are and who believe in themselves go out to defeat the enemy.

If enough members of the Church begin to believe in themselves, to see themselves as God sees them, the devil is in trouble. We will chase him out of the United States, catch up with him in the Philippine Islands and blow him out of there, then chase him out of the Communist-dominated countries. He is not going to have anywhere to go but the Pit. But we cannot do that as long as we think we are insignificant worms who are just waiting for Jesus to come quickly and take us out of this old sinful world. Jesus does not need us to fight for Him in Heaven. He needs us here.

We are not going to be the victorious, glorious Church without spot and wrinkle until we begin to believe in ourselves. The problem of sin in the Church will fall away when enough Christians begin to believe in themselves. Mighty men and women of valor do not go to bed with people to whom they are not married. They know they are too important to lower themselves to such behavior.

On the other hand, we are not going to get the sin condition straightened out by saying, "You are a no-good, low-down dog, and you are going to Hell."

If you believe you are no good and "low down," you will figure you might as well go on sinning. But if you see that you are a mighty person of valor who is too good for that kind of lifestyle, and too important for that kind of behavior, and too special to God to stoop to those kinds of conditions, you will stop doing those things. You will not get rid of drug and alcohol habits by thinking of yourself as stupid and dumb. That kind of thinking does not lead toward freedom but toward suicide.

To be free, you need to realize that you are a champion and champions do not need alcohol and drugs to be powerful and strong. Champions do not need tobacco. Sin will drop off when you begin to see yourself as God sees you.

There is a story about a royal family who were Christians, but the people rebelled and cut off the heads of the king and queen. But they thought killing was too good for the young prince, and they turned him over to a witch who was to lead him into sin.

They said, "If we kill him, he will go to Heaven, and that is too good for him. Let the witch teach him how to be a sinner. Then when he dies, he will go to Hell." (The enemy always hates the people of God and tries to pervert them if he cannot destroy them.)

The prince was turned over to the witch, who tried to lead him into sin. The first thing she did was try to teach him to curse.

But he said, "No. I am a prince. I do not talk that way."

She tried to teach him other sinful things, but he would say, "No! I will not be involved in such behavior. I have royal blood."

*Knowing who he was kept him from sinning.*

You need to know who you are in order to become part of Gideon's army, the band of three hundred. Do not worry or fear or become involved in sin.

You have "royal blood" in you, and there is nothing for you to fear. After all, the sword in your hand is yours and God's. How can you lose with God as a partner?

# 4
# Believing in Yourself

Be ye transformed by the renewing of your mind.

Romans 12:2

...Forgetting those things which are behind.

Philippians 3:13

Resist the devil, and he will flee from you.

James 4:7

During my years of ministry, I have found six hindrances that keep Christians from joining Gideon's army. These problem areas keep people from believing in themselves as children of God and as co-wielders of the *sword of the Lord*. We will discuss three of those areas in this chapter and the other three in the next.

## Negative Programming
## That Has Not Been Replaced

All of us grew up in different environments with different information programmed into our souls through the conscious and subconscious minds. This input from those around us — family, friends, and school — determines how we think for the rest of our lives.

Our homes, of course, are the primary environment. Our parents taught us the way we think today. Most of them did not realize they were teaching us *how* to think, but that is the end result of the attitudes and behaviors we absorbed as we grew up. It was not what our parents said that affected us, usually, so much as the way they acted. Much of the training most Christians have received was negative. Our parents were not evil or bad or trying to do something wrong. They just believed negative things and, consequently, taught us negative things.

Some people have had things such as, "You kids are trying to drive me crazy," drilled into them. They began to believe they drove other people crazy. They never thought that consciously, but inwardly, they believed it. Therefore they act out that belief with their mates, their bosses, and their children. They are miserable and make everyone around them miserable because of being trained as very small children that they drive people crazy. That may sound odd, but it is true.

Then others were taught things like, "If you are not good, Jesus will not love you."

That is an evil teaching and deceptive way of thinking to insert into a little child's mind! If we tell our children that Jesus does not love them when they are not perfectly good, we are lying! God loves us no matter what we do. That lie is a manipulative tool some parents use to force children to obey through a sense of fear and guilt. But what it really does is make God into an ogre and turn the children against Him. That concept gives children an impossible goal. No one can be good enough to earn God's love. His love is a free gift, given out of His everlasting mercy, not because we deserve it.

Parents who program their children in that manner do it because that is how they themselves were taught. They grew up believing that God could not love them because they did not measure up to His (their parents') standards.

Whether you realize it or not, you learned to think a certain way — to have certain attitudes and beliefs — because of words people sowed into your mind. Most of the basic, formative outline of your thinking came from your parents, or from the people who surrounded you from birth to school age.

Most of us were reared on adages such as these: Don't expect too much out of life. You win some and you lose some. It is not whether you win or lose, but how you play the game.

Those are all lies. None of those sayings are based on the Word of God. They sound good, and most of us still believe them and do not even realize we have all those wrong thoughts. People get out of life what they expect, so when a child is told, "Don't expect much out of life," he is being condemned to a mediocre life. He will get only what he expects.

All of us still have a lot of wrong thinking from our early years stored away in our subconscious minds, our memory banks, that dictates much of our behavior. Some husbands and wives learned to shut themselves off from other people through being told or shown that, although people *say* they love you, they cannot really be trusted. So they keep their cars in their own name, keep their own checking accounts, and make sure their spouses pay half of everything. Perhaps even more important, they are stingy with their thoughts and feelings where their spouses are concerned. Without true openness and vulnerability, there can be no true unity.

All of these things are patterns of thinking with which most of us have been programmed. Until those ways of thinking are changed, we will never feel good about ourselves. The sad thing is that most of us go through life and never even think about these things. We cannot understand why we have "hangups," or why we are not what we see in some other Christians, or why we get involved in sinful things or hurtful behavior. We keep on doing things we know we ought not to do and do not know why. Because of all the negative programming we received as children, we end up feeling badly about ourselves.

When I went to school and was put in a certain class, I was told, "You are average."

The Bible word for average is "lukewarm," and God spits out that kind of Christian. In God's family, every child is special. There is no "average" with God. Everyone has special talents with God, but the world teaches us that we are "average."

It is just as bad for children to learn that they are in the "fast class" or the "slow class." Children in the slow class are programmed with the thought, "You are slow. You are the lower half of the class."

There is hope, however! *You can change any thought any time you want.*

You can wake up and think, "I hope I get through this day halfway decently."

On the other hand, you can change that thought in a split second and say, "I am going to make this the best day I have ever had."

You can decide what your thoughts will be — *as a man thinks, so is he.*

Programmed negative thoughts keep you from believing in yourself and can limit you throughout your entire life. But you can change them in a split second and begin to believe in yourself and to live the life God has planned for you. Do not be molded by the world. Do not live the way the world lives. Do not think as the world thinks.

> **And be not conformed to this world: but be ye transformed by the renewing of your mind, that ye may prove what is that good, and acceptable, and perfect, will of God.**
>
> **Romans 12:2**

How can you transform your mind from low self-esteem to high self-esteem? How can you transform your life from poverty to prosperity? How can you transform your life from sickness to health? How can you transform your life from depression to joy? By the renewing of your mind!

You can do the will of God only to the degree that your mind has been renewed. If your mind is a little renewed, you can do the good will of God. If it is a little more renewed, you can do the acceptable will of God. If you renew your mind to a great degree, you can do the perfect or mature will of God. The key to doing God's will is how you think.

Somewhere that negative chain from parent to child must be stopped. Christians must start thinking

God's thoughts and putting His thoughts into their children. How do you get God's thoughts into your children? By getting them into yourself first.

Begin with how you think about yourself, then renew the thoughts you have about those close to you to the way God sees them. If your thoughts are positive, you will begin to believe in yourself and to live the kind of life God has planned for you.

## Carrying Guilt From the Past

Another reason many people do not believe in themselves is because they carry their pasts around with them. They have little suitcases on wheels full of past failures attached to their belts, and everywhere they go those bags of failures are dragged behind them. Carrying the past will keep you from believing in yourself and accomplishing God's plan for your life.

> Brethren, I count not myself to have apprehended: but this one thing I do, forgetting those things which are behind, and reaching forth unto those things which are before,
>
> I press toward the mark for the prize of the high calling of God in Christ Jesus.
>
> Let us therefore, as many as be perfect, be thus minded: *and if in any thing ye be otherwise minded,* God shall reveal even this unto you.
> Philippians 3:13-15

That was the apostle Paul speaking. If anyone had *apprehended,* it should have been Paul.

But he said, "I have not got it all yet. But this one thing I do (one thing, the most important thing to Paul). *Forgetting those things which are behind, I move forward to the things which are ahead.*

God is not basing His plan for your life on your past failures. Any time you bring them up or think of them, you have stopped thinking about God's plan and started thinking about Satan's plan for you. Carrying the past — the guilt, the fear, and the bad feelings — will keep you from fulfilling His plan. But until you cut that little suitcase loose, you will not know what His plan for you is.

> **Remember ye not the former things, neither consider the things of old.**
>
> **Behold, I will do a new thing; now it shall spring forth; shall ye not know it? I will even make a way in the wilderness, and rivers in the desert.**
>
> **Isaiah 43:18,19**

How do you get to the rivers and to the way of God? By remembering not the former things. God wants to do new things in your life. If you carry the past with you, you will be limited forever.

Some of us have big suitcases, full of family things that go way back. We carry grandpa, great-grandpa, and great great-grandpa along with us.

"Great-grandpa had a temper, grandpa had a temper, my daddy had a temper, and I have always had a temper. I guess I always will. It just runs in the family."

But God said, "Forget those things which are behind."

You may say, "Are you not interested in your heritage?"

Yes, I am. My heritage is in the Lord. I cannot win from past successes, and I certainly cannot win from past failures. I forget those things that are behind. The only thing on my mind is the prize Jesus has waiting for me — the prize of the high calling.

If you are thinking about the past, how much faith can you exercise?

Hebrews 11:1 begins, **Now faith** *is* .... If you are thinking of the past, you cannot exercise faith, because faith is now, not in the past. Most people have more faith in the past than they do in what the Word of God says.

Many Christians carry guilt from what they have done or guilt and anger because of what was done to them. Those things keep people from believing in themselves. No matter how bad those things are, they are already done. Why carry them with you all your life?

Once when I was a teenager, I stayed with my grandparents who lived next to a cemetery. That cemetery had a nice road around it which made a good race track for motorcycles. So my friends and I raced around the graveyard. Some skunks lived in the graveyard, and one of them tried to cross the road in front of a motorcycle. For a while after that, my grandparents did not want me to stay with them; the neighbors did not want me to visit; no one wanted to be around me. That was bad enough — but it would have been worse to have picked up that skunk and carried him with me everywhere I went.

You may have done some things or had some things done to you that were bad, but it will not help matters to pick them up and carry them with you. Forget those things which are behind.

## Allowing Satan's Negative Thoughts Into Your Mind

You may say, "I have forgotten all of my past. I do not have problems from back then, and I have renewed my mind from everything that was wrong."

That is fine, but you still have an enemy who is trying to keep feeding evil into your mind. The devil talks to us through his demon spirits, angels who fell with him from Heaven. But he also talks to us through the ways he has established in the world.

Look at the ways God talks to us — through books, television, tapes, the Bible, billboards, sermons, and other people, as well as through the still, small voice of the Holy Spirit. The devil has to communicate in the same way. He sends you messages through billboards, magazines, television and radio programs, videos and songs, as well as thoughts dropped into your mind by passing demons.

Satan is only one being. He is not omnipresent nor all powerful. But his troops come at us in many different ways. That means you have to be ready to resist.

**Submit yourselves therefore to God. Resist the devil, and he will flee from you.**

**James 4:7**

If you were resisting the enemy in an earthly war, you would have to be ready to resist airplanes, missiles, submarines, ships, troops, germ warfare, and propaganda. You would have to be ready to resist that enemy in many different ways. If he knew you had a strong resistance where airplanes were concerned, he would attack you in ships. With the same tactics, the devil comes at you in a lot of different ways, and many Christians are not prepared to handle them. We have not put up our guards. The actuality of our enemy has not been real to us. Because of that, we do not stay strong, confident, and powerful in the Lord. We are vulnerable to the enemy's attack.

One of the main ways the devil attacks is through negative words. These words may come through people around you. You may get yourself fired up Sunday morning, but on Monday you have to go to work. You may try to resist some of the negative talk going on around you, but perhaps by Wednesday you have let down your guard and are right in there telling dirty jokes with the rest of them. That is not resisting! The negative words they are sharing are birthed in evil, negative, satanic things.

Perhaps the talk is not about sex but politics. Pretty soon you are into strife and contention with someone of a different political party, and you end up angry and resentful. Then you wonder why you lack spiritual strength when someone in your family needs healing or when you and your wife have difficulties.

You tend to be upset at God then and say, "Why can't we overcome? We have prayed and believed the Word. God, why aren't You answering our prayers?"

You have allowed Satan into your life, and he has robbed you. Now you have no strength to withstand his attacks.

When you go to work, you have to make a decision not to let the devil work through the people around you to pull you down. Make a decision not to listen to wrong things and not to be led into arguing. Find some Christians to share with, and witness to the worldly people. Love them and share the love of God with them.

But tell them, "My ears are not garbage cans, and my mouth does not spill out trash."

Are you submitted to God and resisting the devil? Then you have to stay away from and resist that negative input. You have to keep your mind clear. Resist the evil word, and doctrine, and message coming at you all the time.

> Above all, taking the shield of faith, wherewith ye shall be able to quench all the fiery darts of the wicked.
>
> Ephesians 6:16

It *is* possible to quench every fiery dart that Satan throws your way. What are the fiery darts? They are the thoughts, the negative messages, the evil teaching that we are exposed to in the world's system every day. You can resist those things if you keep the shield of faith in front of you. Faith is confidence in God's way not the world's way. Faith believes God's Word, not the world's word. When you keep the shield of faith up high in front of you, anything that is not of faith will hit it and fall off.

Someone may say, "Interest rates are going up again, and the economy is going to be terrible."

If you keep the shield of faith high, you can say, "I do not receive that. I resist that because God has already told me that all my needs are met according to His riches in glory. They are not met according to the economy or the strength of the dollar."

If you do not resist, you will catch yourself worrying about money. The fiery dart of the wicked one will stick right in your mind, *if* you do not resist it.

Or the devil will come by and say, "The Hong Kong flu is in town."

If you do not hold up the shield of faith and say, "I do not worry about any kind of flu because by the stripes of Jesus I am healed," you will start to worry about getting sick. Pretty soon you will begin to check yourself to see if you are getting the flu and find yourself saying, "Oh, that feels like what they said would happen. I think I have one of the symptoms. Yes! There it is."

You have to resist that. You have to keep that negative input out of your head. Many of us allow all that to permeate our minds until we never get to the place where we really believe in ourselves, or know the confidence that God has in us, or experience the strength in Him that God says we have.

Second Corinthians 10:4 says, **For the weapons of our warfare ....**

Warfare? Warfare? Many Christians would say, "What are you talking about, warfare? I got saved to be peaceful."

But many Christians have been defeated without ever knowing they were in a fight.

> (For the weapons of our warfare are not carnal, but mighty through God to the pulling down of strong holds;)
>
> Casting down imaginations, and every high thing that exalteth itself against the knowledge of God, and bringing into captivity every thought to the obedience of Christ.
>
> 2 Corinthians 10:4,5

You have tens of thousands of thoughts every week. Every one of those must be captured and made obedient to Christ. Most people are not even aware of what they are thinking, so it is no wonder they lose so many battles in life. Paul said Christians are fighting a war, and we have to use God's weapons to tear down imaginations.

God's weapons are the sword of the spirit, the shield of faith, and the other armor He has given us. (Eph. 6:10-18.) With those weapons we are to tear down the strongholds in our minds. If we do not capture our thoughts, if we do not bring into captivity every thought to the obedience of Christ, we will lose the war. We have to make sure that Satan does not feed negative thoughts into us. How do you do that? First you have to recognize negative thoughts, then you have to pull them down.

Sometimes we avoid those thoughts so fast that we can convince ourselves we really did not think them. Your mind works so fast that you will rationalize and excuse yourself for something you did to the point that you will actually believe you did not do it.

Capture that thought and say, "Here is the thought I now have, and right now, in the name of Jesus, I repent."

It may try to come back, but fight it and say, "I do not think that way. I refuse it in the name of Jesus."

If you really want to stop Satan from sowing evil thoughts and negative thoughts into your mind, then you begin to think on positive things. Philippians 4:8 says we are to think on things that are true, honest, just, pure, lovely, of good report, virtuous, and praiseworthy. If there *is* any virtue, or any praise of God, we are to think on those things. Do not spend all day trying to resist evil. Spend all day thinking of the good, and when the evil comes, capture that thought, repent of it, resist it, and get back to the good.

We must stop allowing Satan to feed our minds with negative influences if we want to believe in ourselves.

We have to stand up and say, "I am going to get my thinking cleared up. I am going to get my mind cleared up, and I am going to believe in myself the way God believes in me. I am going to think about myself the way God thinks about me. No one is going to control me, and no one is going to make me feel badly. No one is going to put me down, and no one is going to stop me from receiving God's best."

When you have that kind of attitude, you are on your way to victory because Satan will *have* to flee. Resist the devil, and he *will* flee from you. (James 4:7.)

# 5

# Competition and Comparison

*...Comparing themselves among them-
selves, (they) are not wise.*

**2 Corinthians 10:12**

*...Then shall he have rejoicing in himself
alone, and not in another.*

**Galatians 6:4**

*...Thou desirest truth in the inward parts.*

**Psalm 51:6**

Three more areas that constitute hindrances to
being able to believe in yourself are comparing yourself to — and competing with — other people,
believing that some thing or some other person can
make you happy, and compromising or rationalizing
away what you know is right.

## Comparing Yourself to, and Competing With, Other People

People who think in a carnal way tend to compare themselves to, and compete with, other people.
The entire world system is based on Satan's desire to
"divide and conquer." He brings about division
through comparison and competition.

People decide what they are going to wear by
comparison with what everyone else is wearing. They
decide what they are going to do by what everyone
else is doing. They decide what music to listen to by
what others are listening to. The world is based on

comparison and competition — but the Body of Christ must be different. We must base our lives on the Word of God.

Galatians 5:19 and 20 lists these things among the works of the flesh: adultery, fornication, uncleanness, lasciviousness, idolatry, witchcraft, hatred, variance, and *emulations*. That last word means "jealousy to the point of copying, or imitating, someone else." It is trying to "keep up with the Joneses." It is being so envious of someone else that you try to be like them.

Paul said Christians should walk in the Spirit. When we do, we will not fulfill the lusts of the flesh. As long as you try to be like others, to emulate them, to compare and compete with others, you will never really believe in yourself. You will never really know yourself, and you will never have confidence in yourself. You will not see yourself as God sees you. You will see yourself as you think other people see you.

You need to stand up and say, "I am going to be me. I am going to live the Word of God and follow the Holy Spirit, and I do not care what any other human being says about it. I do not care if they like it or if they do not like it. I do not care if they agree or disagree, this is the way I am going to be. I am not going to be jealous, and I am not going to copy others. I am going to do what God called me to do."

Emulation is a very powerful stronghold, a powerful tool of the devil. A lot of people will never have God's best because they are too worried about what other people will think about them. They emulate those around them and miss God's best for their own lives. The Corinthian church apparently was permeated with this kind of thinking because Paul specifically addressed it.

> **For we dare not make ourselves of the number, or compare ourselves with some that commend themselves: but they measuring themselves by themselves, and comparing themselves among themselves, are not wise.**
>
> **2 Corinthians 10:12**

When Paul talked about those that "commend themselves," he was talking about being puffed up, about having pride and being arrogant. He was not talking about having an innate sense of your worth in the eyes of God. He was talking about gaining a false self-worth by comparing yourself to others. When we begin to compare ourselves with other people, we become foolish. Children of God are supposed to compare themselves with Jesus. He is to be our goal, our vision, and our example. We are to be like Him. When we become jealous, envious, and competitive, we show ourselves to be very unwise. That is a demeaning position in which to live. Anyone who is always comparing himself to others will never feel good about himself.

There will always be some who are not as good at certain things or not as physically attractive as we are, and there will always be those who are better than we are at those things and more physically attractive. Any time you compare yourself, there will be some who fall below you and others who are above. It is a "no-win situation." You cannot feel good about yourself while you are putting other people down, and you cannot feel good about yourself while you are putting yourself down!

There is only one way to believe in yourself and to have the self-worth, confidence, and self-esteem that God wants His children to have, and that is to put everybody on common ground. You need to realize that everybody is equal in God's sight.

Jesus says I am supposed to love you as I love myself. If I am putting you down, what does that do to me? We must have everybody on common ground if we want to believe in ourselves and have the power God wants us to have. As long as we have people categorized according to race, class, gender, or social position, we will never be free to believe in ourselves.

> **For as many of you as have been baptized into Christ have put on Christ.**
>
> **There is neither Jew nor Greek, there is neither bond nor free, there is neither male nor female:** *for ye are all one in Christ Jesus.*
>
> **Galatians 3:27,28**

## Believing That Someone or Some Thing Can Make You Happy

This could be called the "if only" syndrome. "If only I had a girlfriend who was blond and five feet seven with blue eyes, I would be really happy"; or, "If only I had a new car."

When I was sixteen, I was absolutely convinced that if I had a Corvette I would be happy. No one could tell me that car would not make me happy. I looked for and found the one I wanted — a burgundy V-8 with a black interior. I *knew* that would make me happy. I believed it with all my heart, so I got it. I drove it and felt good for about three days. Then the wheels were not right.

I thought, "If only I had eight-inch ET mags and L-60s on the back with six-inch mags on the front, I would really be happy."

So I worked and worked and got the wheels. Then I had to put air shocks on because the first day out I scratched up the white letters on the tires. Finally the car was looking good — for about a week. Then what I really wanted was a Holley four-barrel with a Tranchella manifold and headers. If I had that I would really be happy. When I got it, I was happy for about a week. Then I wrecked the car.

The point is that *no thing* and *no other person* can really make you happy.

How many people get married thinking their mates are going to fulfill their lives? But it does not work because no person can fulfill your life. Many marriages end in divorce in this country because a man or woman thinks the other person is going to make them happy. Then after six months or a year or five years, they find that other person has not made them happy. Instead of realizing that their expectations were unrealistic and false, most of them go right on looking for the "right" person, the one who will make them happy.

Other people place their hope for happiness and fulfillment in money. They think, "If I just had a bigger income, I would really be happy. If I could get that car, or that house, or that yacht, I would be happy. If I could go on that cruise or get that place in the mountains, I would be happy. If I could go to Europe. If I could wear the latest fashions," and on and on.

But those things would not really make any difference in their inner lives. Once they got used to having them, the lack of peace and happiness would surface again. Most people in those situations do the same thing as those who divorce looking for greener pastures. They go looking for more things to make them happy.

Why do so many film and television stars overdose on drugs, commit suicide, go through several divorces, or end up with cancer, tumors, or ulcers? They have all those things that many people think will bring happiness — physical appearance, money, and fame. They have tried everything they believed would make them happy, and none of it worked.

> **A good man out of the good treasure of the heart bringeth forth good things: and an evil man out of the evil treasure bringeth forth evil things.**
> **Matthew 12:35**

Where is the self-worth, the self-esteem, the confidence and strength to see yourself as God sees you, going to come from? It comes from your heart. You will *bring forth* good things. You *can* have rejoicing in yourself alone. True self-worth comes from within and not from without.

> **But let every man prove his own work, and then shall he have rejoicing in himself alone, and not in another.**
> **Galatians 6:4**

True self-esteem must be an inner assurance. It cannot be gotten from your husband or wife, from a job or career, from talents and abilities, or from money. You cannot even get it from God. You have to get it for yourself from yourself. God will not *make* you feel good. If He could without overcoming your will, He would have straightened you out a long time ago. God will not force you to be happy. Happiness comes from resting in Him. Have rejoicing in the Lord alone and not in another person. Anything you get from another person is temporary.

## Compromising or Rationalizing Away What You Know Is Right

Many people have the mistaken idea that renewing the mind means learning new things. But just knowing something is not good enough. Knowledge in itself is not effective. Many Christians think getting closer to God simply means knowing more about Him. However, you can know everything it is possible to know about God and be a million miles away from Him. Knowledge in your head is not enough. That knowledge has to be translated into your behavior and your actions in order to do any good. It has to become part of your everyday life, a way of living.

If we started doing everything that we already know to do, most of us would be super Christians. We would be bold and powerful. Why are we not like that? The last area of our thinking that can keep us from becoming what God wants us to be is compromise and rationalization. We cannot feel good about ourselves when we know in our spirits that we are rationalizing wrong actions, compromising what we know is right, and excusing ourselves for doing both.

In the first three chapters of Revelation, Jesus dictated to the apostle John letters to seven churches in Asia, and in one of them Jesus addressed this kind of problem.

> And unto the angel of the church of the Laodiceans write: These things saith the Amen, the faithful and true witness, the beginning of the creation of God;
>
> I know thy works, that thou art neither cold nor hot: I would thou wert cold or hot.
>
> So then because thou art lukewarm, and neither cold nor hot, I will spue thee out of my mouth.
>
> Because thou sayest, I am rich, and increased with goods, and have need of nothing; and knowest not that thou art wretched, and miserable, and poor, and blind, and naked:
>
> I counsel thee to buy of me gold tried in the fire, that thou mayest be rich; and white raiment, that thou mayest be clothed, and that the shame of thy nakedness do not appear; and anoint thine eyes with eye-salve, that thou mayest see.
>
> Revelation 3:14-18

Jesus was saying, "You look good. You sound good, and you really think you have it made, but in reality, you are lukewarm."

God does not want us lukewarm, or moderate. He wants us to be either hot or cold, either for Him or against Him. We have taken one admonition that Paul wrote to the Philippian church and blown it so far out of proportion that we should be spanked every time we quote it!

> Let your moderation be known unto all men.
>
> Philippians 4:5a

God does not want us to live a moderate life. If you stay moderate (lukewarm), He is going to spew you out of His mouth. We are not to have a moderate life where He is concerned. There *are* certain kinds of actions in which we are to be moderate, but in our attitude toward God and in our spiritual lifestyle, we are to be hot.

The Greek word translated as *moderation* in the *King James Version* does not mean moderation in today's English. In *The Amplified Bible*, that word is translated "unselfishness." It also could be translated "considerateness." Both those words are a far cry from what we think of today when we hear the word *moderation*.

In James 5:16, we read, ... **The effectual fervent prayer of a righteous man availeth much.**

"The red-hot prayer of a righteous man accomplishes much" is another way of expressing James' thought. You are not supposed to be a mediocre and moderate pray-er. You are supposed to pray fervent prayers. When you pray, tear down the strongholds of the devil.

In Romans 12:11, Paul wrote, (Be) **not slothful in business;** *fervent in spirit,* **serving the Lord.**

That means to be "white hot," which is hotter than red hot. The Holy Spirit inspired Paul to write to Christians to be fervent, white-hot, and totally committed in the service of God. We need to get out of mediocrity, to move out of moderate living, to go all the way for the Lord. We need to believe the Word, act like God, talk like God, and think like God. We need to go all the way all the time, no matter what the situation. If you do that, you will find the power of God ready to flow right out of your life.

Careful, moderate, lukewarm, and mediocre Christianity is nothing more than religious tradition, and God will not accept it. Doing things "decently and in order" (1 Cor. 14:40) does not mean being wishy-washy or a "wimpy" Christian.

You may say, "But I just want to have a normal Christian life."

That is exactly what I am talking about — what God says is the *normal* Christian life.

"But what about all these other Christians? They seem to be more normal — quiet, no fanaticism, minding their own business."

Churches full of Christians who are not making an impact on the community are not God's norm. They are mediocre and lukewarm in the eyes of God. What is normal in the sight of the world is subnormal in the eyes of God. To the multitude, God's normalcy is fanatical. In God's opinion, the normal Christian is like the apostles of whom it was said they turned the world upside down.

> And when they (the Jews which believed not) found them (Paul and Silas) not, they drew Jason and certain brethren (those who had received the apostles) unto the rulers of the city, crying, These that have turned the world upside down are come hither also;
>
> Whom Jason hath received: and these all do contrary to the decrees of Caesar, saying that there is another king, one Jesus.

**And they troubled the people and the rulers
of the city, when they heard these things.**

**Acts 17:6-8**

Any time you are red hot for God and go
around proclaiming that Jesus is king, it will turn
your part of the world upside down and trouble the
people and the rulers. Notice also that it was the religious people, those who believed in God, who were
the most offended and who stirred up the secular
world. Not compromising the testimony of Jesus and
the Word of God may bring some degree of persecution; nevertheless, that is the normal Christian life.
That is the kind of life God wants us to lead.

Young converts usually operate this way. They
are what "settled" Christians consider "wild." They
will call up their friends and say:

"Glory to God, want to hear me talk in tongues?
That is what you need, brother. Come on over here, I
have a new language I want you to hear."

But after we have been saved for a while, we
become "wise and proper." We are concerned about
offending other people. In other words, we start
becoming lukewarm and dead.

God wants us on fire. John the Baptist said that
Jesus would baptize with the Holy Spirit and fire.
(Matt. 3:11.) Most Christians are like charcoal, not like
fire.

When I learned to ride a bicycle, I was taught
that you cannot steer it until it starts moving. Once
you take off on that bicycle and are rolling down the
road, you can steer in a certain direction. That is the
way Paul operated. One time he was in Antioch with

some other believers, and they were praying, fasting, and seeking God when the Holy Spirit spoke to them to lay hands on him and on Barnabas for the mission field.

While the two men were en route to a certain place, the Holy Spirit spoke and said, "No, do not go that way."

Then they started for Asia, and the Holy Spirit again steered them by saying, "No, not that way either."

After a night's sleep, the Holy Spirit gave them a vision to go to Macedonia.

Paul and Barnabas had their bikes rolling so that the Holy Spirit could steer them. The problem with the Church is that many Christians are sitting back waiting, instead of getting in motion.

They are saying, "Lord, what do You want us to do? What is Your will, Lord? We are just seeking You, Lord."

But they are not doing anything. They are being moderate and not moving. Being lukewarm is depressing. It is a miserable lifestyle. Being moderate is being average. It is a sad place to be, and that is why a lot of people fight depression, worry, and bad feelings. That is why they cannot feel good about themselves. They are lukewarm.

Of course, if you are red hot and moving, you may do some things wrong. But you will feel good about all the things you are doing right and be able to straighten out the things you do wrong. Look at Moses. In his early and later years, he was anything but moderate. It was only in those in-between years of his life when he ran away from trouble and exiled himself in the wilderness that he became moderate and accomplished nothing for the Lord. Look at what is written of him in the Lord's Faith Hall of Fame.

> **By faith Moses, when he was come to years, refused to be called the son of Pharaoh's daughter;**
>
> **Choosing rather to suffer affliction with the people of God, than to enjoy the pleasures of sin for a season;**
>
> **Esteeming the reproach of Christ greater riches than the treasures in Egypt: for he had respect unto the recompence of the reward.**
> **Hebrews 11:24-26**

Moses set out to go all the way, even if he did get sidetracked later for a while. In his zeal for the Lord, He did get ahead of God's timing and tried to deliver the children of Israel in his own might. But because of that zeal and commitment to God, the Lord was able to use him later. Moses became a mighty man of valor for the Lord not because of his forty years of moderation in the desert, but because of his early determination to move out and to do something. His red-hot years made it possible for God to use Moses in a great way later.

He said, "This worldly lifestyle does not matter to me. I am going all the way, and if I have to lose my home and my royal rank, it does not matter. I would rather have God's best than the pleasures of sin for a season."

*The Amplified Bible* translates another comment about Moses in his later years this way:

> [Motivated] by faith he left Egypt behind
> him, being unawed and undismayed by the wrath
> of the king; for he never flinched but held
> staunchly to his purpose and endured steadfastly
> as one who gazed on Him Who is invisible.
>
> **Hebrews 11:27**

Do not be satisfied to settle for a lukewarm, mediocre lifestyle for a season. There is a little fulfillment, a little satisfaction out there in sin or in mediocrity, but if you will go all the way with God, you will find a lot of satisfaction and fulfillment. Be committed to the Lord and believe in yourself enough not to flinch or to get worried and upset over all the earthly things that come against us. We need to hold staunchly to God's purpose and to endure steadfastly because we have *Him Who is invisible* living within us, while Moses could only look on Him outwardly. We have advantages that Moses did not have under the old covenant.

If you go all the way for God's best, you will begin to feel good about yourself. You will find self-worth. You cannot find self-worth and then go act on it, however. You must act on it, and then find self-worth. Stand up for what you know is right without being awed or dismayed by those around you, and then you will find the strength, courage, and confidence to stand.

Each time you do not stand up for what is right, a little of the self-esteem you do have is eroded away. You get beaten down a little more. Each time you stand up *in love* for what is right, you get stronger and become a brighter light for the world to see.

Compromise and rationalization almost destroyed David. He was king of Israel, and everything seemed to be going great. God was blessing him, but he fell into adultery and then murder. He had killed many people in defense of Israel, but causing the death of Uriah was his only murder. His compromise with what he knew was right almost destroyed his whole life. His actions brought much confusion and trouble to the kingdom of Israel.

David wrote Psalm 51 after being confronted by the prophet Nathan who had brought out all the sin and compromise with which David had become involved.

> **Behold, thou desirest truth in the inward parts: and in the hidden part thou shalt make me to know wisdom.**

> **Restore unto me the joy of thy salvation; and uphold me with thy free spirit.**
> **Psalm 51:6,12**

When David rationalized the truth, compromised, and got off into sin, he lost his joy. David lied to himself.

God wants us to be honest with ourselves. No one around us knows the situations and things that we go through every day. The only one who knows what is going on inside you is you. That is where you have to start being clean. You have to start being righteous on the inside. Stand up for what you know God would have you do, and that is where you will find joy. Then the joy of your salvation will be restored unto you.

# 6
# A Blueprint for Life

The mind of every human being has two parts, and those parts operate differently. There is a part of the mind that operates like a robot. This part is where we have our beliefs and our attitudes. This is where we have what we call our subconscious responses and programs. We usually are not aware of this part of our mind. It is just there functioning all the time.

In your "robot mind," you might have the belief that you are a bad reader. You may never consciously think that about yourself, you just *know* that you are. Your robot mind will make certain that you behave according to the programming that it has.

When you begin to read, you are motivated by that unheard program that says, "You are a bad reader. You do not do well because you are a slow reader."

The other part of your mind is what I call the "judge mind." This is the rational, reasoning, conscious thinking part of your brain. However, it does not matter what the judge says — what we do is whatever has been programmed into the robot.

The judge can be saying, "This is what you need to do. This is what is going to be best. This is what is going to bless you. This is what is going to have you walk in God's best," but the robot does not even hear that reasoning.

The consequence of this conflict is that you find yourself doing things and wondering why. The conflict for a Christian comes because the robot is programmed with the world's ideas and beliefs that have been fed into it since birth, while the judge mind has been learning the wisdom and understanding of God since the second birth. The two mind sets are opposite for the most part. The result is that you do what you do not want to, and do not do what you want to. Many people are frustrated in their spiritual lives because of this problem.

Sitting in church and hearing good teaching feeds the judge, but it does not change the robot. Learning is not renewing. Learning can make the judge smart, but it does not do anything for the robot. The robot mind could care less what new and contradictory information you take in, because it is still in charge.

*Renewing the mind* does not mean simply taking in new facts. It means to examine yourself and see the beliefs, the concepts, and the attitudes that really control the way you live. Then you must meditate, confess, and exchange that old programming for what the Word of God says. That does not happen through sitting in a pew at church. It is accomplished through daily prayer, and through meditation, concentration, and purposefully exchanging old ways of thinking and old beliefs about yourself and the world for new ones.

*Gaining knowledge is not renewing the mind, and you must be transformed by the renewing of your mind before you can do the will of God.*

## An Example of Subconscious Programming

Suppose you were brought up attending church regularly, and you were taught (with the appropriate punishment to reinforce the programming if you forgot) that when you got to church you were to sit down, be quiet, and take a nap until church was over. Your family never sat on the front rows. What happens today when you go to church? As soon as you walk into the church, you lower your voice. The closer you get to the front of the sanctuary, the quieter you get. You sit at least four or five rows back, perhaps way in the back. You do not plan on doing anything in church but sitting there. If anyone says "amen," you are offended. You just sit there and listen quietly. It does not matter if you understand what the preacher is talking about or not. You are not there to get anything. You are just there. That is the way you have been programmed and the way you believe church should be.

Then one day you go to a church where they are participating in praise and worship. They read admonitions from the Bible such as "Lift up your hands. Shout unto God with a voice of triumph. Dance before the Lord with all of your might."

Immediately your little robot says, "Wait! Hold it! Red alert! Mayday! Mayday! No, you cannot do that in church. You can do that at the sports stadium. You can do that in the bowling alley or the roller rink, but not in church."

Many times, that is the last time a person so programmed will attend a church like that. But he will never know why he was so offended. Many times, he will justify or rationalize his reactions away on religious grounds.

He will say, "I think that is blasphemous. True religion is quiet and decent and not in disorder. That kind of church service is irreverent."

Did the Word of God have anything to do with his reactions? Did a hunger for God have any part in them? No. That person arranged his knowledge and his beliefs in order to protect and maintain his robot mind. It is unsettling, of course, to upset the status quo and begin changing. It feels like swimming upstream, because God's ways are flowing opposite or contrary to the world's ways. But your robot will override your hunger for God, if you do not renew your mind by changing all those old programs.

Some people recognize that the Bible says one thing and their feelings another (the programs of the robot mind are expressed consciously as "feelings," not emotions but "feeling a certain way"), but they rationalize the Bible away in order to protect the programming. Admitting your "programming" is in error is admitting that you are wrong about something, and many people have difficulty ever admitting that they have been wrong.

Such a person may say, "I can see that it is in the Bible, but I do not feel as if I can ever do it."

So he comes to church and watches everyone else doing what the Bible says week after week after week. He is not about to act on the conscious thinking and rational knowledge of his judge mind because his robot mind says:

"Don't you dare! If you do, I will fight you and make you feel bad and out of order. I will protect myself at any cost."

The robot mind will override even the Bible. It does not reason, but can only feed back what has been fed into it. What makes it dangerous is that the robot mind controls behavior. Usually we act certain ways and then justify and rationalize and defend our actions, instead of questioning them to find out what wrong programs are in our minds.

If you do not want to renew your mind — if your robot has too strong a hold on you — it will not matter what you can see plainly in the Bible. It will not matter that you can read it for yourself. The only thing that matters is what that little robot is telling you. Until you get the robot in line, the judge is not going to make a bit of difference. Old negative programming keeps you from believing in yourself and from having complete confidence in yourself.

## The Robot Mind Empowers the "Old Man"

Paul said, "Take off the old man which is corrupt."

**But ye have not so learned Christ;**

**If so be that ye have heard him, and have been taught by him, as the truth is in Jesus:**

**That ye put off concerning the former conversation the old man, which is corrupt according to the deceitful lusts;**

**And be renewed in the spirit of your mind;**

**And that ye put on the new man, which after God is created in righteousness and true holiness.**

**Ephesians 4:20-24**

That old lifestyle is full of deceit, corruption, and negative, deceitful desires. All of those are in that old man. Paul said to take that off and put on the new man which is created in righteousness and true holiness. To the Colossians, Paul said the new man is created in the image of God. (Col. 3:10.)

How do you take off the old man and put on the new one? By becoming renewed in the **spirit of your mind.** The "spirit of your mind" is that little robot. Paul was not talking about the conscious thoughts that go through your mind every day. We dealt with those in the last two chapters. What Paul is talking about is the underlying *pattern* of the way you think, the bottom-line attitude that controls your life. That is what must be renewed. Otherwise you can learn and learn and listen to tape after tape, read the Bible, read books, and still not get anywhere with God.

## People Perish Without a Vision

**Where there is no vision, the people perish.**
**Proverbs 29:18**

I realize that visions given by God are very remarkable and supernatural. If Jesus appeared to you and talked with you, you would be having a vision. Some people have had visions of being taken out of the body and transported to Heaven. But I want to talk about a vision in the definition of "goal, dream, plan, or desire." The vision Christians must have is not one given supernaturally by the power of the Holy Spirit but one birthed into their spirits — a realization of God's plans for their lives.

Your desire, plan, or goal makes up your vision. **Where there is no vision, the people perish** does not mean that unless you have a supernatural experience, you will die. It does not mean that if the clouds do not burst open and you see Heaven, you will not make it. It means if you do not have a goal, a desire, a dream, a plan, or a purpose in your life, *then* you are going to miss out on God's best.

> **Delight thyself also in the Lord; and he shall give thee the desires of thine heart.**
> **Psalm 37:4**

I believe the verse has a two-fold meaning. First, I believe it means that God *puts* a desire in your heart. He may give you the desire to play some musical instrument, or the desire to get people born again through your business, or to produce Christian television shows and movies, or to write books that will spread the Gospel. I believe God puts those desires in people. I do not think people dream things like that up on their own.

The other meaning of Psalm 37:4 is that whatever you desire, God will give to you. He put the desires there, and He will bring them to pass. The desire in your heart is the vision that you have for your life. Without such a desire, or vision, people perish spiritually. If you have nothing to live for, you will die. Hopelessness results from a lack of such a vision. A person who has no vision for his life, no reason to live, and sees nothing but darkness ahead will be susceptible to suicidal thoughts.

The Hebrew word translated *perish* has to do with being scattered abroad and put in confusion. Many Christians are confused today and wandering around as sheep without a shepherd. Of course, the world stays in that condition, but Christians are not supposed to live that way. Many of us, however, are confused and do not know how to deal with the affairs and circumstances of life.

We could also express the concept like this:

Where there is a negative vision, a negative desire, or a negative goal or plan, people live negatively.

At one time in my earlier years, I spent time in the county jail because I had a negative vision for my life. There are many Christians living in sickness and poverty today because their visions are of sickness and poverty. People who have positive visions will live positive lives. The way you see life, the vision you have for yourself, controls the way in which you live.

Everyone has such a vision, either good or bad. It came from the Word or from the world, the kingdom of the devil or the Kingdom of God. Those are the only two places where we can get visions for our lives.

If your vision is from the world, it usually has to do with fun, money, sex, fleshly satisfaction and gratification — fame, fortune, and power.

From the Word of God, your vision is for love, joy, peace, and prosperity in every realm of life — spirit, soul, and body. From the Word of God, you can get a vision of success spiritually, mentally, physically, and financially.

Although we are born again and even filled with the Spirit, many of us still carry the worldly vision in our thoughts. Our outlook on life, our goals, dreams, and desires are still from the world rather than from the Word. Many times we have to make a conscious effort to change that vision and get it lined up with the Word of God. When we do, we will begin to enjoy the abundant life that God has to offer.

In the Church, many act as if they "have it all together." We act like the apostle Paul's right-hand man or as if we are the next best thing to Jesus. That attitude is *not* evidence of self-worth or true self-esteem. True self-worth shows in the way you describe yourself when no one is around. When you do not have anyone to impress or to keep a facade of pride up for, how do you feel about yourself?

If someone walked up to you and said, "I can see your body, but I cannot see your spirit and soul. Describe them to me," what would you say?

Would you say, "I am just getting started," or "Scared and confused"? Would you say, "Bold as a lion," or "Bold as a lion *by faith?*" The way you describe yourself when you do not look good for someone else is the vision you have for your life. When you are honest and tell the truth about how you feel about yourself, then your vision for your life comes clear.

You need to recognize exactly where you are, so that you can know what to change. Otherwise, you are like a person with a map who does not know where he is in order to start. If you do not know where you are, what good is a map?

"There is where I want to go, but I do not know how to get there because I do not know where I am now."

Be honest and take a look at your vision of yourself. How do you really see yourself? Not how you see yourself when you are making faith confessions — that is where you want to go. But to get there, you have to be honest about your starting point.

You have to say, "Okay, here is where I am. This is what I am going to do to change my direction. This point over here is where I want to go. This is the area of my vision that has to change in order for me to reach the goal."

## Your Vision Is Your "House" Plan

Your vision for yourself is like an architectural drawing or a house plan. When an architect designs a house, he puts rooms where he wants them and makes the rooms the size he wants them. He lines everything up and makes it one or two or three stories, or a split-level. He decides whether to have a basement or an attic. Then he gets everything drawn out and arranged on paper. After that, the electrical drawings, the plumbing drawings, and other aspects are added. Then he gives all of the plans to the builder. The builder does not create the vision of the house — the architect did that. The builder puts together the vision that the architect had. Those pages of the blueprint are the vision.

If the architect goes over to the lot after the house has been constructed and says, "That is the ugliest thing I have ever seen," whose fault is it? His own. He cannot blame the builder.

What kind of architectural renderings do you have for your life? If you do not like the kind of life that has been constructed up until now, guess who is responsible? The plans that were used to construct your life were inside your own head. If you do not like the building that has been constructed, talk to the architect — you.

Your parents had input. Your school teachers had input. Your community and church had input. All that different input has affected your life throughout the years. But the fact remains that *you* took all of that, put it together in your mind, and developed the life which you are now living.

It does not do any good to get mad at mom and dad or anyone else and say, "If only ...." That is not going to change where you are today. Begin to change the vision, the blueprint of your life, and a few years down the road, you will get a remodeled version. That "house" will be lined up the way you wanted it to be.

Many of us have ended up in circumstances that we did not like, but instead of adjusting our visions, we tried to adjust everyone around us. We tried to straighten out our wives or husbands. We tried to straighten out the children. We tried to straighten out the neighbors. We tried to straighten out our pastors. We even tried to straighten out God.

Many people have done everything but say, "Wait a minute. Maybe I need some changing. Maybe I need to make an adjustment in my vision. Perhaps I need to change the way I see myself. Maybe I need to get in line with the Word of God."

The devil can bring evil circumstances, but we are in control of how we respond to those circumstances. People may do some very negative things to us, but we are in control of how we respond and what we do about those things. We are the master architects in charge of the visions for our lives.

**O generation of vipers, how can ye, being evil, speak good things? for out of the abundance of the heart the mouth speaketh.**

**A good man out of the good treasure of the heart bringeth forth good things: and an evil man out of the evil treasure bringeth forth evil things.**
**Matthew 12:34,35**

In terms of the architect illustration, we could paraphrase those verses this way:

"O generation of vipers, how can you, being evil, speak good things, for out of the plans in your hearts, you will create your lives. A man with a good plan will bring forth a good life. A man with a negative plan will bring forth a negative life."

Notice who Jesus said was "bringing forth" the life. He did not say, "God will bring forth good treasures." Nor did He say, "The devil will bring forth evil treasures." He said a good *man* and an evil *man*. People bring forth the things in their lives. Who brought forth the things in your life?

Many Christians think the Lord did the things in their lives, and that they could not help what has happened to them.

People have actually said, "The Lord got me and my wife divorced. He did it."

Others say, "The Lord put me in the hospital."

If you have good things in your life, you brought good things forth. If you have bad things, you brought bad things forth. If you have a messed up marriage relationship, guess whose fault it is? It is not the dog's fault. It is not the children's fault. We have to reach the point where we realize that everything is not up to God or the devil.

God gave you a will and said, "Go and take dominion. You live your life, and you bring forth good things."

It is wrong to blame everyone else for what is going on in our lives. We can submit to God and give our lives to God, but we are still responsible for our lives. We can submit to the devil and give our lives to the devil, but we are still responsible for what goes on in our lives. *We* bring forth good things, or *we* bring forth bad things.

In my own life, I grew up with a vision that I was "not good enough." I do not know what "good enough" was, but I was not it. Because I thought that way about myself, I spent much of my time trying to convince whomever I was around that I was really okay. What I was really trying to do, of course, was convince myself. I would say things I did not believe, if I thought someone would like it. Maybe then, I would be good enough. I would do things I did not want to do, because then someone might like me and I would be good enough. I would not say the things I really thought or do the things I really wanted to do. I was afraid someone else might catch on to the fact that I was not good enough. That kind of vision can destroy your life.

All of us respond to those kinds of programming in different ways. Some people with a poor self-image get real tough and mean. They become bullies. Many of those who walk around acting real tough are actually scared to death inside. They are putting on a tough act so no one will see they are afraid. Other people are shy for the same reason — a bad self-image.

*Peer pressure* is able to affect an entire generation because people have grown up feeling badly about who they are. They feel they are not "good enough," so they walk around trying to do what everyone else is doing in order to fit in and be good enough to join the crowd. That vision — always trying to do something so people will like you — can destroy a person's life.

So how do you become a winner by simply being yourself? You begin by getting a dream for your life and then dreaming of winning.

# 7
# Six Ways to Develop Your Blueprint

**What things soever ye desire, when ye pray, believe that ye receive them, and ye shall have them.**

**Mark 11:24**

Christians need to develop "blueprints" for themselves based on the Word of God. They will not succeed with one built on some feeling picked up from the world as a result of peer pressure. Nor will dreams succeed that are based on what parents have said (in their own thinking and not from the Lord), or what school teachers have said, or what friends think.

Developing that vision based on the Word of God does not mean just reading the Bible or hearing the Word. You can memorize nine thousand scriptures, go to church seven days a week, and listen to tapes all the rest of the time, but if you do not change the vision on the inside of yourself, you will never reach the place God has planned for you. When you begin to develop that positive vision of God's plan for your life, then the good man inside of you will bring forth good things.

A story I heard about a Seattle businessman is a perfect example of these principles.

When this man was a very young child, he had infantile paralysis for which there was no medical treatment at that time. Within a few ι nths, the boy was retarded and crippled. His legs were useless. His family did believe in God and in His Word, but like many Christians today, they did not expect their prayers to be answered.

Not knowing what else to do with the boy, they placed him in a wooden box on the floor that his mother could drag from room to room with her as she worked. She set a mirror in front of him so that he could entertain himself in the box.

One day a few years later, this boy looked in the mirror and had a vision. He saw himself running around, completely healed. Jesus appeared to him and told him that he would be able to walk and run. That vision dropped supernaturally into his heart. Even with a supernatural vision, however, the boy had his part to do. If he had just sat in his box wishing he could run and play and waiting for God to drop the healing manifestation in his lap, his vision would have been useless.

He exercised his faith in the vision by doing what he could day by day. At first, he learned to rock the box so it would fall over. Then he would use his arms to pull himself out of the box and begin scooting across the floor. His mother would pick him up and put him back in the box, but he kept rocking it all day long. He had a vision of getting out of the box, and he was putting "legs" to his vision. He did that for months. Pretty soon, he could scoot faster than his mother could get to him. Before much longer, he could get over to a chair, pull himself up, and get his legs underneath him.

He kept doing that day after day, week after week, month after month, and as a teenager, he was able to walk. Then he became able to run. By the time he was a young man, he walked and lived as a normal human being. Without being told, no one could know that he had spent his early years in a box. He became a very prosperous and successful businessman.

The vision in his heart got him out of the box. When his mother came to put him back in, his vision would rise up and say, "No! You are not going to keep me in a box."

Dr. Kenneth Hagin of Tulsa, Oklahoma, as a bedfast teenager not expected to live, got a vision of complete healing from reading Mark 11:23,24, and he followed his vision by exercising faith every day although he could not at first exercise his body. Those verses are good foundations for any vision or dream.

> **And Jesus answering saith unto them, Have faith in God.**
>
> **For verily I say unto you, That whosoever shall say unto this mountain, Be thou removed, and be thou cast into the sea; and shall not doubt in his heart, but shall believe that those things which he saith shall come to pass; he shall have whatsoever he saith.**
>
> **Therefore I say unto you, What things soever ye desire, when ye pray, believe that ye receive them, and ye shall have them.**
>
> Mark 11:22-24

Some of us have been in a financial box, and people have said, "You are going to be in a box all your life."

If you sit there believing that and saying, "I guess that is true. I do not deserve any more than this. I guess God wants to keep me humble," you *will* stay in the box.

We need to rock our boxes. But when we start falling out of them, not everyone around us is going to like it. They may try to put us back in the box. If you want to do anything with your life, however, you had better start rocking.

Say, "Thank God, I will not be in debt all my life. I am going to prosper. I am going to have an abundance of finances, and I will not have to pay mortgage bills. I will not have to borrow money. God will bless me with abundance. I am going to get out of this financial box, so that I can give liberally into the work of the Lord."

When you do that, count on someone else saying, "That faith stuff doesn't work. Get back in your box."

Other people have accepted illnesses or diseases as permanent situations. They need to begin seeing themselves well and healthy. They need to climb out of those limitations. Rock the box, and get out of that rut.

Christians have allowed themselves to accept less than the best in every realm of life. Let's take a look at what God says about us instead of what the devil says about us. We need to find out that God loves us and calls us His children. He looks at us as *more* than conquerors. He looks at us as overcomers, as pearls of great price. We are created in His likeness and image, and His children hold the highest place of any other creatures in the universe, right below the Father.

The Bible says that when we believe on the Lord Jesus, we are raised up and seated with Him in Heavenly places, not below Him. The Bible says that we are heirs of God and joint heirs with Jesus. We are not sub-heirs nor lower heirs, but joint heirs. Everything that Jesus has, we have. All that Jesus inherited, we inherit. Jesus placed us in authority over the whole earth.

We have said, "We are just hanging in there. We are stupid and unworthy, but we are praying for mercy. We will never do much, but if we could be of some small help to this generation, we would just thank the Lord for that."

We thought that if we ever said, "I can do all things," that would be pride. That is not pride, that is spirituality. That is believing the Bible.

We thought if we said, "I tread on serpents and scorpions, and nothing shall by any means hurt me," we would be boasting. That is not boasting. That is seeing ourselves as God sees us. That is agreeing with our Father.

Christians must develop a vision of themselves according to the Word of God, if we are to win the world for the Lord. We need to bring out of the treasure within ourselves the real man and woman that God has created. We must start by developing a positive vision.

Following are six things that will help you develop a vision for your life.

## Search Your Heart for Your True Desire

Many times we get confused while looking for our own true desire. We may see someone else's dream and try to make it ours.

Some people see a pastor and say, "That has to be the best job in the world. He only works Sundays and Wednesday evenings. The rest of the time, he does his own thing. He drives an expensive car and wears great clothes. He is respected in the community. That has to be a great job."

That is a totally unrealistic view of a pastor's life, of course. But because they see someone else doing something that looks good, they get a desire to also do that. But that desire is of the mind, not of the heart. It is not in line with the plan that God has for them. So they begin to follow someone else's dream and have problems. They will not succeed but have trouble. They stumble and fall, then get mad and give up.

Another way people can develop a false dream or vision is doing what others think they should do.

"Mama always wanted me to be a nurse," or "Dad told me I should be a doctor."

Trying to live on what others say instead of what is in your heart will never bring success. In Psalm 37:4, God said He would give us the desires of our hearts, but remember that has a twofold meaning. He will give us the desire in the first place, and then fulfill it. Find the desire of your heart, and you will be on your way to getting that dream fulfilled.

## Know That Your Desire Is God's Will

Is it God's will for the thing you desire to happen? Does God want people to prosper? Does God want successful businessmen? Does God want strong, powerful teachers? Does God want dedicated pastors? Yes, of course he does, but you must settle once and for all whether one of those things is God's will for *you*.

You need to know without any question or doubt that you are doing God's will for your life.

> **And this is the confidence that we have in him, that, if we ask any thing according to his will, he heareth us.**
>
> **1 John 5:14**

You say, "How do I know if my dream is God's will for my life?"

First of all, what is your desire? Is it in line with the Word? It is very easy to see that a desire to be a prostitute or a successful thief is not one of God's chosen occupations or callings, but what about running for public office? Search the Word, and you will find that God is for good government and for godly government officials.

Secondly, if God does not in some way specifically let you know that you are going in the wrong direction, then you must be doing what He wants you to do. A good indication of His will is whether you have peace in your heart about what you are dreaming or doing.

> **But if ye have bitter envying and strife in your hearts, glory not, and lie not against the truth.**

> This wisdom descendeth not from above, but is earthly, sensual, devilish.
>
> For where envying and strife is, there is confusion and every evil work.
>
> But the wisdom that is from above is first pure, then peaceable, gentle, and easy to be intreated, full of mercy and good fruits, without partiality, and without hypocrisy.
>
> James 3:14-17

If you have peace about what you are dreaming, and if the fruits are good, then you can be sure your dream is from God.

## Get Agreement and Input From Others

Not everyone will like your dream, but you need someone to share with. Being out there on your own will bring you problems. Even the Lone Ranger had someone to agree with him. If you cannot find anyone to agree with you — not even your own spouse — your dream probably is not valid.

> Again I say unto you, That if two of you shall agree on earth as touching any thing that they shall ask, it shall be done for them of my Father which is in heaven.
>
> Matthew 18:19

> Where no counsel is, the people fall: but in the multitude of counsellors there is safety.
>
> Proverbs 11:14

Many people start out to do things without getting counsel, without talking about their plans with others in the Body of Christ, and they get hurt and in trouble. If they had just talked their plans over with a pastor or with family and friends, they could have avoided a lot of trouble. Find someone to agree with you.

Spiritual discernment plays a part here, obviously. You will have to be able to discern which advice is good counsel and which advice comes from envy or doubt or the world's wisdom. Also, usually, counsel from godly counselors will confirm what the Lord has already been showing or saying to you.

## Write Down Your Vision Plainly and Simply

In the early Sixties, a pastor in Korea began to write down a figure on a piece of paper. The figure was "150." He had a vision of one hundred and fifty people coming to his church. Before the end of the year he reached that goal, although many times, it had looked as if he was not going to make it. Then he kept increasing his vision. Right now, the Rev. Paul Yonggi Cho pastors a church with more than half a million members. How did he start? He had a dream, then he wrote it down and made it plain.

Writing down your dream helps you to become organized and to see the things that need to be done to bring that dream to pass.

## Speak Your Dream Out Loud

You need to speak your dream out loud. Dr. Cho began to confess his dream out loud, and the more he heard himself say it, the more he believed it. He also began to thank the Lord that the dream was true. Mark said **whosoever shall *say* and whatsoever he *saith*** (Mark 11:23). If you do not say it, you will not have it.

When people get mad because of my dream as they did with Joseph, it lets me know I am on the right track. People do not say anything bad about churches that are not doing anything. No one throws mud at their signs or speaks badly of their pastors or spreads lies about them. When you begin to talk about your dream, you are going to stir up the devil. But you have to speak your dream aloud, if you believe it is real and of God.

> **We having the same spirit of faith, accord-ing as it is written, I believed, *and therefore have I spoken*; we also believe, *and therefore speak*.**
>
> **2 Corinthians 4:13**

## Patiently Endure Until the Dream Comes to Pass

The desire that God places inside of you is *powerful*. Tradition and religion often associate human desire with evil and corruption. Many Christians believe that if they really want something, it must be of the devil. If they want it, it must not be God's will. They believe that God's will for them is whatever they do not like and whatever they do not want, but that is not true. The reverse is true, many times, however. The soul of man is in conflict with the reborn spirit, and will rebel against what God wants, so many Christians do not like and do not want what God wants for them. But if you are truly committed to doing the will of God and have the "robot" section of your mind renewed to God's ways, then your desires will be in line with God's will.

The Bible says that the desire of the righteous is good. When you desire good things you release powerful energy and creativity. Your desire for good is God's desire being expressed in and through you. God placed Adam and Eve in an environment of abundance, happiness, health, and fulfillment before they sinned and lost that perfect dwelling place. God has never changed His mind about what He wants for His people. God desires for His children to live in the best circumstances possible.

God loves you and desires good for you. You were born to live in God's dream and in His lifestyle. When you recognize the Holy Spirit within and realize that God's will for man has never changed, you will begin to dream a new dream. You will begin to desire what He desires for you. Have faith in God's dream for you. Faith is your desire turned toward God, and faith has power.

# 8

# Winning Begins
# With a Dream of Winning

**Delight thyself also in the Lord; and he
shall give thee the desires of thine heart.**
**Psalm 37:4**

Winners start being winners by dreaming of winning. We have been created in the image of God, and because God gives dreams, we can develop dreams. Whether you call dreams for your life "visions, hopes, desires, goals, or plans" does not matter — you start achieving things in life by dreaming.

There are several different kinds of dreams, of course. There are dreams given sovereignly by God, such as Joseph's dream in the Old Testament. There also are dreams that we develop ourselves.

A lot of people are in situations they do not like and wish they were not there. They have unpaid bills, physical problems, situations with children, or businesses in bad shape. They are where they are because the dream of yesterday was what they have right now.

You say, "Oh, no, they certainly did not want that!"

I did not say they *wanted* it. I said present circumstances were what they had in their minds. You

111

may not like that idea, and you may not accept it, but it is still true. *You are today what you dreamed yesterday.*

When I was in high school, I was afraid to graduate because I did not know what I was going to do. I knew how to skip the classes and still get by, but I was going into the world where a note from my parents would not take care of things anymore. I was scared because I had no vision or dream and thought I was "not good enough." I could not see myself doing anything.

I began to say, "If I could just get a job and get by, I would be all right."

I found myself washing cars and getting by for two or three years. I started at $1.25 an hour and worked my way up to $1.32! I would get my paycheck and spend it on what I wanted, then that was the end until the next week when I got the next paycheck. Why was I in that spot? Because that was my dream. That was my only vision, my only plan, and that was all I got.

On the other hand, I had a friend who was very smart and could do everything well. He was studying to be a doctor while I washed cars. I was learning how to get tar off a fender, while he was learning all about the human body. Why was I washing cars, and why was he in medical school? Why was I sitting in jail a couple of years later when he was practicing medicine? Why were people calling me "stupid" and him "doctor"? We had gone to the same school and had gotten the same grades. We had the same country, the same state, and the same opportunities. But I was a failure, and he was a doctor. Why? Because I had dreamed of barely getting by, and he had dreamed of becoming a doctor. Both of us were living our dreams. Where you are today is the result of the dreams you had in the past.

Psalm 37:4 says, **Delight thyself also in the Lord; and he shall give thee the desires of thine heart.**

When you delight yourself in the Lord, He will give you the dreams of your heart. Psalm 37:5 goes on to say, **Commit thy way (dreams) unto the Lord.** If you do not have a positive goal or dream, you have nothing to commit to the Lord, and there is nothing that He can bring to pass.

God is giving many people the desire of their hearts, but their hearts are so empty that they really do not have much desire there.

If you asked some people what their goals are, they would say, "If I could get my rent money together, I would be happy," or they might say, "I would like a bigger house."

God wants you to have a home. But if a house is the goal of your life, your vision is pretty small. If your only dream is to have the skins of a bunch of little critters hanging around your shoulders, your life is pretty shallow. Life is more than houses, mink coats, and cars, but those are the only things some people dream for — a new car, a new house, more property, and to get away from it all. God has more for you than that.

What about a dream of helping people? What about a dream of going to other countries and sharing the Gospel? You do not have to be a preacher to do those things. You can do them as a businessman or woman. What about a dream of having such a prosperous business that you can travel around and minister to people? What about holding seminars to teach Christian people how to win? What about influencing nations by speaking to presidents and to kings and queens about Jesus?

God wants to give you the desires of your heart, but you have to develop those desires. A desire of the heart is real and life changing. It will influence and help other people. You have to have a dream in order to win in life. Without a dream, you are bound for failure — "a born loser."

Why do many marriages break up as soon as the children leave home? Because the parents only had a vision of staying together until then.

Why do many people die or become invalids right after they retire? When they retire, it is possible for them to work full time for the Lord. They can travel and do all the things they always wanted to do, but then they get sick and die. Why? Because their vision only lasted until retirement, and then it was over. Their dream ended, and when it was fulfilled, they died. People without dreams are dying all over the world.

Why is the world so wrapped up in tranquilizers and amphetamines? People take a pill to go to bed and a pill to get up. Why? They do not have a dream to get them going. They have no motivation. They do not know why they are alive. They think the whole world is an accident. They have no reason to live, and they are perishing.

God wants us to have a positive dream, a positive life, and an abundant ministry. You can have an abundant life if you have a dream from the Word of God, a dream He has brought to life for you from the Word. You will be strong, prosperous, and able to help people.

## Every Dream Has Conditions

The prophet Elijah had a helper, a servant named Elisha. This assistant to the prophet served him for many years. Elisha carried water, cooked, held the prophet's coat, opened his door, delivered his messages, and generally took care of his business. Although he was only a servant, Elisha developed a dream. He had a vision for his life and a goal. When it came time for Elijah to leave this world, Elisha's goal was within his reach.

> It came to pass, when they were gone over, that Elijah said unto Elisha, Ask what I shall do for thee, before I be taken away from thee. And Elisha said, I pray thee, let a double portion of thy spirit be upon me.
>
> 2 Kings 2:9

Notice that Elisha did not hesitate. He had been dreaming. He knew what he wanted from the prophet.

He did not say, "I am going to have to pray about this," or "But, Master, I am so unworthy."

He said, "I want a double portion of your spirit. I want twice as much."

All those years, whenever he saw Elijah call fire out of Heaven, Elisha had said to himself, "I want twice that much." When he saw Elijah raise the dead, he had said to himself, "I want *twice* that much, I want a double portion."

But there were conditions to be fulfilled before his goal was attained. You cannot just sit around and hope that what you have dreamed will fall out of Heaven upon you. Elisha had to do something in order to get his dream fulfilled.

First, he had to be tenacious and cling to his dream. He had to not let himself be discouraged from pursuing his goal. Elijah set out the conditions in his answer.

> **And he said, Thou hast asked a hard thing: nevertheless, if thou see me when I am taken from thee, it shall be so unto thee, but if not, it shall not be so.**
>
> **2 Kings 2:10**

Several times, Elijah tried to discourage him as the two men made that final journey.

Elijah would say, "Wait here, I will be right back," or "You can stay here, Elisha."

But Elisha would reply, "I am staying right with you. I have been dreaming this dream too long to let it get away from me now. I am going to get the double portion."

When the Lord has given you a dream, you have to be willing to do whatever is necessary to make it come to pass. Look at what happened to Elisha.

And it came to pass, as they still went on, and talked, that, behold, there appeared a chariot of fire, and horses of fire, and parted them both asunder; and Elijah went up by a whirlwind into heaven.

And Elisha saw it, and he cried, My father, my father, the chariot of Israel, and the horsemen thereof. And he saw him no more: and he took hold of his own clothes, and rent them in two pieces.

He took up also the mantle of Elijah that fell from him, and went back, and stood by the bank of Jordan;

And he took the mantle of Elijah that fell from him, and smote the waters, and said, Where is the Lord God of Elijah? and when he also had smitten the waters, they parted hither and thither: and Elisha went over.

2 Kings 2:11-14

Elisha's dream came to pass because he was willing to go as far as necessary to see it happen. He would not let the prophet Elijah out of his sight that day because he had a dream. His dream had kept him a faithful servant to the prophet from the time Elijah called him out of the field where he was plowing.

God has given the believer power, authority, and dominion on this earth. As a believer and a child of God, you have the right to develop a dream and to go for it full blast. A lot of Christians are sitting around waiting on God, but God is waiting on us. He is not going to tell us everything. God gave us minds and free wills. Why would He give us wills that enable us to make choices and decisions if He is going to do everything for us? He gave us minds to reason, to think, and to plan.

117

Many of us have the wrong idea when we say, "I am just going to let the Lord lead me."

Instead of meaning that we ask the Lord for His guidance and trust Him to lead and direct us, we somehow take that to mean that God is going to carry us up the path. *Being led by the Holy Spirit* does not mean for you to do nothing. Remember the bicycle? You begin to move and the Holy Spirit will tell you "full speed ahead," or "watch out for the curve," or "there is a trap ahead," or "you are going the wrong direction."

God is waiting for you to develop a vision and to go on and start living it out. He is not going to tell you every little detail that you should know for yourself.

## Your Dream May Make Other People Angry

A word of warning: when you begin dreaming dreams, not everyone else is going to like it. Some people are going to get mad at you for dreaming a dream. They may actually hate you and persecute you. But do not let that stop you or slow you down. Other people may think your dream is silly. They may think it will never work. But if it is truly a dream in your heart and you are sure it is from God, then go for it!

In the Old Testament, we read of a man named Joseph, who had a dream. It was given him by God in the night hours, but the reactions of the people around him were the same as reactions of many people today to those who have dreams of the heart. Joseph was the great-grandson of the patriarch Abraham and the beloved son of Jacob, later called

Israel, the father of the Israelites. But did his ten older brothers appreciate his dream? No. When he first told the vision he had in the night, even his father made fun of him.

> And Joseph dreamed a dream, and he told it his brethren: and they hated him yet the more.
>
> And he said unto them, Hear, I pray you, this dream which I have dreamed:
>
> For, behold, we were binding sheaves in the field, and, lo, my sheaf arose, and also stood upright; and, behold, your sheaves stood round about, and made obeisance to my sheaf.
>
> And his brethren said to him, Shalt thou indeed reign over us? or shalt thou indeed have dominion over us? And they hated him yet the more for his dreams, and for his words.
>
> And he dreamed yet another dream, and told it his brethren.... (When people get mad at you for dreaming, go dream another dream!)
>
> And he told it to his father, and to his brethren: and his father rebuked him, and said unto him, What is this dream that thou hast dreamed? Shall I and thy mother and thy brethren indeed come to bow down ourselves to thee to the earth?
>
> **Genesis 37:5-10**

When you "dream" a dream, many people may get mad at you, and a lot of their anger comes from envy. Those people wish for dreams of their own. They envy another person who can dream. But they will never do anything but wish, and wishes never produce any results.

When you begin to dream, circumstances are going to come against you. The devil does not want your dream to be fulfilled. Whatever kind of dream it is — financial, ministerial, family-related — the devil is going to try to stop you. He will come against you with circumstances, trials, and tribulations. He will use Christians, the government, or whatever else he can. But continue to dream your dream!

Joseph went through many circumstances. However, after being thrown into a pit, after becoming a slave, and after being in prison for several years, his dream came true. He became ruler of the entire nation of Egypt. There came a day when his brothers had to come to him for food and help, and they bowed down to him exactly the way his dream had shown. Even his father had to come to him for help. How did it all start? With a *dream*. Joseph's part in all that was to remain true to the Lord in the midst of adverse circumstances, not to give in to the doubt and self-pity of Satan, and to do his best and what was right in all of the situations.

The Holy Spirit dwelling within you is all you need to have a dream or a vision and to see that thing come to pass. Develop a dream, and God will bring it to pass.

# 9
# Building a Positive Vision

**O ye dry bones, hear the word of the Lord.**
**Ezekiel 37:4b**

There are five steps you must take in order to build a positive vision for your life. Remember that we saw from the life of Elisha that every dream has conditions to be fulfilled? Five of those general conditions are these:

Meditating on the Word of God, speaking only the Word about yourself, writing the vision, keeping your mind on the vision, and acting on the vision.

## Meditate on the Word of God

*Meditating on the Word of God* is another way of saying "renewing your mind."

First of all, to meditate on the Word of God means to not put a lot of ungodly things into your mind. Do not take counsel of the ungodly nor stand around and idly talk with sinners. Do not spend time listening to those who are scornful of the things of God. The first psalm deals with this very clearly.

**Blessed is the man that walketh not in the counsel of the ungodly, nor standeth in the way of sinners, nor sitteth in the seat of the scornful.**

**But his delight is in the law of the Lord; and in his law doth he *meditate* day and night.**

> **And he shall be like a tree planted by the rivers of water, that bringeth forth his fruit in his season; his leaf also shall not wither; and whatsoever he doeth shall prosper.**
>
> **Psalm 1:1-3**

We need to be aware of what is going on in our minds in order to have positive visions. In the first verse of Psalm 1, we are told *what* to put in our minds. In the second verse, we are told *how* to put it into our minds. In the third verse, we are told what will be the result *if* we put the right things into our minds.

That psalm advises you not to even think about anyone who is ungodly or a sinner or scornful of the Lord. Do not think about what they are saying or what they are doing. Stay away from that type of involvement, unless you are witnessing to them of the Lord or taking an opportunity to stand up for the things of God and for your faith. In that case, they should be listening to you and not you to them. Keep all the negative input from the world out of your mind. Christians need to guard what goes into their minds.

You may say, "That is really narrow-minded."

You are right. Jesus said, "The way is narrow that leads to life."

If you do not want to be narrow and in the way that leads to life, you can be broad-minded. But Jesus also said, "The way is broad that leads to destruction."

To *delight in the law of the Lord* literally means "in the ways of the Lord" or "in the truth of the

Lord." The person who is blessed has his mind on the things of the Lord all the time.

Some people think that in order to be meditating on the Word, you have to be quoting the *King James Version* of the Bible or praying in tongues all your waking hours. Reading and quoting the scriptures and praying in the Spirit are part of meditating, but you cannot do those things all of your waking hours.

*Meditating on the Word day and night* means that your mind is in line with the principles and ways of God all the time. It means that you do not let bitterness have a part in your life. You think about loving and helping people and about being kind to people. You do not get jealous or involved with anger. You build up and encourage other people. You have faith, confidence, and giving to others foremost in your mind. You do not let fear, mistrust, condemnation, and guilt have any place in you. You keep the positive things of God's Word in your mind day and night.

If you want to win and to reach God's best, if you want to be a mighty man or woman of valor, you have to get your mind straightened out and think on positive things.

Psalm 1:2 says, **His delight is in the law of the Lord.**

That is where a lot of people have problems. They have the attitude that attending church is a duty and a responsibility. Saying, "I missed church for two weeks now, guess I had better go," is not being very delighted. A lot of people say, "I know I should go because I made a commitment, so I will do it," and then wonder why they do not receive anything when they go.

You have to be delighted in the things of God. You have to be stirred up or "turned on" about them. *You have to like the things of God.* Many people cannot understand that. The first step toward bringing that dream into reality is getting excited about the ways of God, the blessings of God, the thoughts of God, the things of God. Keep your mind on loving and being kind to other people — and be happy about it! Jesus told the disciples at the Last Supper how they could be happy — by doing the things they saw him do.

> **If ye know these things, happy are ye if ye do them.**
>
> **John 13:17**

We need to be happy, delighted, and excited about the things Jesus said to do. Then we will start receiving some of the benefits.

Joshua said to meditate day and night in the book of the law. He did not say, "Meditate on God's Word in the daytime, and at night, think about whatever you want," nor did he say, "Meditate on the Word of God whenever you feel like it or have a few extra minutes."

> **This book of the law shall not depart out of thy mouth; but thou shalt meditate therein day and night, that thou mayest observe to do according to all that is written therein: for then thou shalt make thy way prosperous, and then thou shalt have good success.**
>
> **Joshua 1:8**

There is a condition to obtaining prosperity and success. Meditate the Word of God day and night in order to do it, *then* you will get the prosperity and success.

A lot of people learn about faith and say, "I am going to prosper. I believe in this faith teaching. I am going to get a new Cadillac. Thank You, Jesus. I am going to get a new job. I am going to get rich!"

But when you ask him if he has been meditating on the Word, he will say, "Oh, I do not believe in that stuff. I am a 'faith man'."

If you ask, "Have you been renewing your mind?" he will answer, "I talked to some people about that, and I am not interested in that 'renewing the mind' stuff. I am just going to prosper."

That person is fooling himself, and the devil's laughing at him all the way to the poor house. God said that you have to get your mind on His Word, and *then* you will make your way prosperous and have good success. If your mind is confused, and you have all kinds of earthly programs in it, you will never get to the prosperity and the success part.

*Meditate* means "to ponder, to imagine, to mutter to yourself, to talk to yourself about, to think, or to picture in your mind." People meditate all the time, even while they are thinking they do not know how to meditate. The only people who do not meditate are those who are so full of drugs that their minds do not function. Otherwise, every person who is alive and breathing is meditating all the time. The problem is that many people meditate on negative things.

They say, "I cannot do it. I just cannot get ahead. I probably will not get the job. I do not know how I am going to get these bills paid. I wonder if my children will get in trouble again today," and so forth.

Psychiatrists say a person has more than ten thousand thoughts every few hours. Thoughts go through your mind at the speed of light. Thoughts go through your mind all day long. The Bible said that every one of those ten thousand thoughts every few hours will have to be in line with the Word of God if you want to ever prosper and have good success — not 25 percent, not 75 percent, not even 99 percent, but 100 percent. Paul wrote to the church at Corinth about this.

> (For the weapons of our warfare are not carnal, but mighty through God to the pulling down of strong holds;)
>
> Casting down imaginations, and every high thing that exalteth itself against the knowledge of God, and bringing into captivity *every thought* to the obedience of Christ.
>
> 2 Corinthians 10:4,5

The human mind operates so fast, yet it can be reprogrammed. Someone said, "You are talking about brainwashing," and that is exactly what I am talking about! Washing your brain with the Word of God. Paul also said the Church is washed with the water of the Word.

> Finally, brethren, whatsoever things are true, whatsoever things are honest, whatsoever things are just, whatsoever things are pure, whatsoever things are lovely, whatsoever things are of good report; if there be any virtue, and if there be any praise, think on these things.
>
> Philippians 4:8

If you will do what that verse says, you will be on your way to becoming the mighty man or woman that God intended you to be. That has to happen if you want to believe in yourself as God believes in you. If you want to accomplish all that God has put before you, you have to meditate on the right things. Get your mind renewed to the Word of God. Get brainwashed with the Word of God.

**It is the spirit that quickeneth; the flesh profiteth nothing: the words that I speak unto you, they are spirit, and they are life.**

**John 6:63**

Jesus said that, but you can quote it and still be all messed up. For the Word to be effective, you must be renewed through the spirit and the life of the Word. Get your mind on the ways of God. Many times people will quote a scripture in order to avoid the truth. Rather than change something, they defend or rationalize it with a Bible verse — the "letter" of the law but not the spirit.

Even the devil quotes the Bible. He came to Jesus and said, "Cast yourself down. God will send the angels to look after you and keep you from getting hurt." (Matt. 4:6.) The devil was quoting Psalm 91:11,12.

But Jesus said, "No, devil. You are speaking the literal words, but not the supernatural Word. Thou shalt not tempt the Lord thy God."

Jesus spoke the supernatural Word to the devil when He quoted Deuteronomy 6:16.

Christians must get their minds in line with the principles and character of God in order to be able to walk in His positive ways.

## Speak Only the Word About Yourself

We must speak only the Word about ourselves, not our doubts and fears. In order to see our dreams constructed into reality, we must speak only what God says about us, not what we have been told when we were younger. We must stop confessing negative things and speak out the good. We must make Jesus our pattern and make the ways of God our ways. God calls those things that are not as though they already are.

> **(As it is written, I have made thee a father of many nations,) before him whom he believed, even God, who quickeneth the dead, and calleth those things which be not as though they were.**
>
> **Romans 4:17**

God called Abraham the father of a multitude long before he ever was. God called Gideon a mighty man of valor long before he ever was. God called Jesus the Savior of the world long before He ever was. God calls things which are not as though they are — and then they become true.

You have to walk in God's principles if you want to have complete confidence in yourself. You may not look like a mighty man of valor. You may not feel like a mighty man of valor. But if you begin to call yourself a mighty man of valor because God calls His children that, before long you will begin to believe it. Then you will become what you say.

You may ask, "But I am not brave and bold. If I say I am, won't I be lying?"

Was God lying when He called Abraham the father of a multitude before he even had one child?

No. God was using His Words to bring things into existence. The Bible says life and death are in the power of the tongue.

> Death and life are in the power of the tongue: and they that love it shall eat the fruit thereof.
>
> Proverbs 18:21

> The wicked is snared by the transgression of his lips: but the just shall come out of trouble.

> A man shall be satisfied with good by the fruit of his mouth ....

> There is that speaketh like the piercings of a sword: *but the tongue of the wise is health.*
>
> Proverbs 12:13,14,18

Get a concordance and run references on *the tongue.* You will gain much insight on its creative power for good and for evil. There is creative power in our mouths. The problem is that many Christians have been creating the wrong things with that power. What are you creating?

When you begin to use your tongue creatively, you may run into resistance from the devil, from others, and from your own mind.

As you begin to say, "I am a mighty man of valor. Thank You, Jesus, a mighty man of valor," your mind may say, "No, you are not! You are undisciplined. Look at yourself. You are a lazy sluggard."

Part of that is from the devil trying to discourage you and put you under condemnation so you will keep a bad self-image, and part of the resistance may be from your own unrenewed mind. But you have to keep saying what God says of you, not what your doubts and fears say. Will you feel like a mighty man of valor? Not at first, but you cannot speak out what you feel. Your feelings will go along with your unrenewed mind. You must learn to speak out the Word.

Doubt will say, "You are never going to get ahead. You might as well forget it. Who do you think you are? You have been negative all your life, and remember all those sins you committed? *You* expect to be prosperous and blessed? Of all people, you do not deserve it."

Then you need to reply, "Jesus redeemed me from the curse of the law that the blessings of Abraham might come on me. I am blessed coming in and blessed going out; blessed in the city and blessed in the field. I am the head and not the tail. I am above and not beneath. I lend and do not borrow." (Deut. 28.)

Call those things which be not (yet) as though they already were in existence. Call your life and your character the way you want it to be. If it does not come out of your mouth, it will not ever happen. Jesus said, "You will have what you say." (Mark 11:23.)

God taught the prophet Ezekiel some marvelous things about speaking things into existence.

> The hand of the Lord was upon me, and carried me out in the spirit of the Lord, and set me down in the midst of the valley which was full of bones,
>
> And caused me to pass by them round about: and, behold, there were very many in the open valley; and, lo, they were very dry.

> And he said unto me, Son of man, can these
> bones live? And I answered, O Lord God, thou
> knowest.
>
> Again he said unto me, Prophesy upon
> these bones, and *say unto them*, O ye dry bones,
> *hear the word of the Lord.*
>
> Ezekiel 37:1-4

What was Ezekiel supposed to do? He was to
*speak* to the dry bones lying out in the valley in this
vision God was giving him. Why did God not speak
to the bones and tell them what to do? Because under
God's plan for His children to have a part in His
work, we have to speak God's Words into the earth.
The Holy Spirit spoke sixty-six books of the Bible but
those books will not have any effect on the world or
on us *unless* some person speaks out with his own
mouth the things God has said.

God said, "Jesus is Lord."

But that will not help you until *you* say, "Jesus is
Lord."

God said, "You can do all things" (Phil. 4:13),
but that will not help you unless *you* say, "I can do all
things through Christ Who strengthens me."

God got Ezekiel to tell the bones to **hear the
word of the Lord.** Under the plan God has set in
motion for His creation, a man has to speak before
the Word will come to pass. Check this principle
throughout the Bible, and you will find it is true.
Even in His pronouncements of wrath and judgment,
God gave His Words to His prophets to speak out
into the earth. Obviously, God does not *have* to do it
that way. He is sovereign and can do what He pleases.

It is His universe, His creation. *But He chose to do things that way from the beginning of the world.* And as God, He can have things the way He chooses! Our part is to study the Word and find out how God operates and then find out what He wants us to say and do.

So Ezekiel spoke to the dry bones.

Thus saith the Lord God unto these bones; Behold, I will cause breath to enter into you, and ye shall live:

And I will lay sinews upon you, and will bring up flesh upon you, and cover you with skin, and put breath in you, and ye shall live; and ye shall know that I am the Lord.

So I prophesied as I was commanded: and as I prophesied, there was a noise, and behold a shaking, and the bones came together, bone to his bone.

And when I beheld, lo, the sinews and the flesh came up upon them, and the skin covered them above: but there was no breath in them.

Then said he unto me, Prophesy unto the wind, prophesy, son of man, and say to the wind, Thus saith the Lord God; Come from the four winds, O breath, and breathe upon these slain, that they may live.

So I prophesied as he commanded me, and the breath came into them, and they lived, and stood up upon their feet, an exceeding great army.

Ezekiel 37:5-10

Today, much of the Church is made up of "dry bones" from all over the world, from every nation, race, and tongue, as well as from all religious persuasions. All those people are lying in the valley. At the same time, a group of people called by God to speak are standing on the edge of the valley prophesying over those dry bones. They are speaking out the words God has given them to say:

"Oh, mighty men and women of valor. Rise up and live! You can pray, and the sick will be healed. You can conquer the works of the devil. You can overcome the world. You can prosper. You can do all things through Christ Jesus."

All over the world there is a rustling and a shaking because those bones are getting up. The flesh is coming back on the bones, the muscles are coming together. The army is rising up. In the last days, there will be a Church full of Holy Spirit-filled people who believe in themselves, who know who they are in the Lord, who are going to be hard on the devil. That Church *will* turn the world upside down.

> So I prophesied as He commanded me, and the breath came into them, and they lived, and stood up upon their feet, an exceeding great army.

> Then he said unto me, Son of man, these bones are the whole house of Israel: behold, they say, Our bones are dried, and our hope is lost: we are cut off for our parts.

> Ezekiel 37:10,11

They were saying their former glory had passed away and did not work any more. They were saying there were no more manifestations of miracles, no more speaking in tongues, no more casting out of demons, no more healing. Hope was lost, and everything was gone. They were cut off. But what did God have Ezekiel tell them?

> Therefore prophesy and say unto them, Thus saith the Lord God; Behold, O my people, I will open your graves, and cause you to come up out of your graves, and bring you into the land of Israel.
>
> And ye shall know that I am the Lord, when I have opened your graves, O my people, and brought you up out of your graves,
>
> And shall put my spirit in you, and ye shall live, and I shall place you in your own land: then shall ye know that I the Lord have spoken it, and performed it, saith the Lord.
>
> Ezekiel 37:12-14

Ezekiel spoke all the things that God said, and they began coming to pass. When you start speaking God's Word about you, it will start coming to pass. You need to talk to situations around you. You need to prophesy to those things. God told Ezekiel to speak to the dry bones.

He was saying, "Do not talk *about* them. Talk *to* them!"

A lot of Christians spend too much time talking about things instead of talking to things. You need to speak to your business and call it blessed, prosperous, and successful. The bones started coming together when the prophet spoke to them. Sinews, muscles, and skin came upon the bones, and finally, life came into the bones.

Some people have homes and families that are like piles of dry bones. But if they begin speaking the Word of God to them, they will change. As you speak to these situations, you create a vision in yourself.

You develop a picture of who you are in God. Eventually, your mind will be renewed. It will not accept negative input from the world and will bring forth only the positive things of God.

## Write Down Your Vision

A lot of Christians have never gotten their visions clear. Their ideas about their personal lives, their homes and businesses, or their ministries are confused, making a fuzzy picture. They are like a man looking for a vehicle who does not know what he wants. He is going to have a tough time, because there are pickup trucks — big ones and little ones, two-seaters and four-seaters, automatics and standard shifts. There are little cars and big cars, cars with small or large engines, cars with leather or fabric interiors. There are whitewall and blackwall tires, mags or hub caps, or no hub caps. There are German, Japanese, English, Italian, and American cars. Then there are all those different colors to pick from! Without a clear picture of what he wants, he will end up with something he does not want.

> **And the Lord answered me, and said, Write the vision, and make it plain upon tables, that he may run that readeth it.**
>
> **Habakkuk 2:2**

Many times, you will not know exactly what to write. That is the first indication that you do not yet know your goal. Once you find out, then you can change where you are. You can build and create your vision into reality by making decisions about where you want to go and what you want to do for the rest of your life. It is sad that so many people attend church regularly and do not realize where they are going in this life. It is like being lost but not being able to find your way because you do not know you are lost! That is a dangerous situation in which to be. The devil can come and destroy you when you are in that state. You are vulnerable when you have no clear direction in which to move.

When you start to write down your vision, then you have to begin thinking about it. To write it down, you have to have things clear in your mind. Ask yourself these kinds of questions:

"What kind of life do I want? What kind of family do I want? What type of Christian experience do I want?"

Do you know what you are doing? Do you know where you are going in life? If you do not know where you are going, how will you know when you get there?

Can you imagine getting into an airplane and hearing the pilot say, "Welcome aboard flight number 49. I do not know where we are going, but I hope you have a nice flight. Just sit back and enjoy yourselves, and the flight attendants will bring you a snack in a few minutes."

If you were on an airplane, you would not accept that. You would have something to say to that pilot in a hurry! Yet in their everyday lives, many people have never taken the time to get a clear picture of who they are in Christ and where they are going *on this earth*. They know their eventual destination is Heaven, but what is the earthly destination God wants for them? You cannot do God's work in Heaven. Here is where He needs you to be a part of

His plan. Do not settle for less than the best. Develop a clear picture of the vision He has for your life.

## Keep Your Mind on Your Vision

The devil would like to steal your vision from you. Mark 4:14 talks about a sower who soweth the word and about all the things that can happen to the word that is sown. Transpose *word* in that verse to *vision* in order to make the point a little clearer.

> The sower soweth the (vision).
>
> And these (believers) are they by the way side, where the (vision) is sown; but when they have heard, Satan cometh immediately, and taketh away the (vision) that was sown in their hearts.
>
> Mark 4:14,15

Satan knows that once your vision is established in your heart, you will start bringing it forth. If he can steal it from you before it gets strong and before you start to birth it into the world, then it will never produce any results. Your dream for your life will go dead and dormant, and you will not receive any of its benefits. So the devil is going to come and lie and steal and do everything he can to get that vision out of you. You *have* to keep your mind on your vision, not on the devil's lies.

> For our light affliction, which is but for a moment, worketh for us a far more exceeding and eternal weight of glory;
>
> While we look not at the things which are seen, but at the things which are not seen: for the things which are seen are temporal; but the things which are not seen are eternal.
>
> 2 Corinthians 4:17,18

When you build a picture of your life based on the Word of God, it is an eternal plan, an eternal vision. The Word of God *will not* fail. If you establish a picture of your life based on the eternal Word of God, it will come to pass.

> **For verily I say unto you, Till heaven and earth pass, one jot or one tittle shall in no wise pass from the law, till all be fulfilled.**
>
> **Matthew 5:18**

You may be in a wheelchair right now, but that is temporary. The Word of God says, **By whose stripes ye were healed** (1 Pet. 2:24).

You may be living in financial poverty right now, but by the authority of God's Word, that is temporary and subject to change. The Word says, "All your needs are met" (Phil. 4:19), and "God will give you the desires of your heart." (Ps. 37:4.)

Your responsibility is to keep your mind on that vision which is eternal, not on temporary afflictions. Most Christians spend a lot of time thinking about their problems. They go over them and over them, tell everyone else about them, and then figure out new ways to express their feelings about all the trouble they have. The old spiritual says, "Nobody knows the trouble I've seen."

But Paul said, "Do not look at those things. Look at what you cannot see — the victory, the vision, the answer, the solution. Look at what the Word of God says, not at what the devil says."

> **Finally, brethren, whatsoever things are true, whatsoever things are honest, whatsoever things are just, whatsoever things are pure, whatsoever things are lovely, whatsoever things are of**

good report; if there be any virtue, and if there be any praise, think on these things.

Philippians 4:8

*The Amplified Bible* translates that verse as follows:

For the rest, brethren, whatever is true, whatever is worthy of reverence and is honorable and seemly, whatever is just, whatever is pure, whatever is lovely and lovable, whatever is kind and winsome and gracious, if there is any virtue and excellence, if there is anything worthy of praise, think on and weigh and take account of these things — fix your minds on them.

What does it mean to *fix your mind* on a particular thing? We all do it in one way or another. A good example for men is when they were young and got their first car, and perhaps for women, it would be their first boyfriend. Whatever it may be — a house, a vacation, a car, or a person — we fix our minds on whatever we want. The things we fix our minds on then absorb our thinking. They are the primary focus of our thought life. So many times, however, Christians fix their minds on negative things — on doubts, questions, worries, and problems. Of course, we do have to consider business, home, and ministry situations and problems daily. But our basic thought life should be fixed on the positive things of our vision, based on God's Word. If you fix your mind on that vision, it will come to pass.

You cannot do this, however, without being in control of your thoughts. The carnal mind will lead you to death. A carnal mind always is thinking on negative things and is full of doubts, confusion, worry, and fear. A spiritual mind is plugged into the vision, the positive plan based on God's ways and God's thoughts. A spiritual mindset will lead you to life and peace.

## Act on Your Vision

After you get your thought life straightened out, your vision firmly established in your mind, and your tongue trained to speak out the vision over the dead bones in your life, then make your actions line up with your vision.

> **But be ye doers of the word, and not hearers only, deceiving your own selves**
>
> **James 1:22**

It is sad to be deceived by someone else, but it is worse to be deceived by yourself. The Bible says that if you hear the Word and do not do it, *you are deceiving yourself!* James said to be a *doer* of the Word. That means to act on it. If you read something in the Bible, act like that. The Bible said God did not give me a spirit of fear, so I will act as if I do not have any fear. Do I ever get scared? Yes, sometimes the devil tries to put fear on me, but I refuse it and act as if I am not afraid. The Bible said God did not give me fear, so I am not going to receive it. You have to act as if the Bible is true in order to make it true in your life.

Before I ever owned a thing, I acted prosperous and talked prosperous. People got mad at me for being rich before I ever owned a car or a house. I was wearing clothes that someone gave me, but I was preaching abundance and claiming it. People would write me letters and say, "It is not right for preachers to be rich." At the time, we lived in a one-bedroom apartment, but we were acting on the Word. There is nothing wrong with anyone being rich, if their substance is dedicated to the glory of God. There is everything wrong with anyone being rich who is using that strictly for carnal purposes and to glorify their own flesh. Money is not the root of all evil. The *love of money* is the underlying cause of all evil, the Word says. (1 Tim. 6:10.)

You have to act on your vision. You have to act like the thing for which you are believing is true. If you are believing God for healing, act as if you are healed. Do not moan, groan, and cry about your sickness. Tears of sympathy never healed anybody. They may comfort your soul and confirm self-pity, but they will not change your sick body. You need the power of God in order to be healed. To have the power of God, you must get established in the vision of health and be acting as if the Word of God is true. Do not be concerned with what other people say. Just be a doer of the Word. Meditate in the Word day and night. Why? So that you will begin to do it. Whether it is easy or hard, whether you feel like it or not, just do it!

> Not every one that saith unto me, Lord, Lord, shall enter into the kingdom of heaven; but he that doeth the will of my Father which is in heaven.
>
> **Matthew 7:21**

The wise man *does* the Word. As you do the Word, you are building a vision of who you are in Jesus. You are developing that picture from a negative to a positive image. The more you do that, the more you establish the vision within your heart. And the more you have the vision, the more it comes forth in manifestation. You bring forth the abundant life from your innermost being.

# 10
# Trust in the Lord Builds Confidence

**For my yoke is easy, and my burden is light.**
**Matthew 11:30**

The pattern of low self-esteem, a low sense of self-worth, or a low self-image can be traced in every negative part of society around the entire world. In foreign countries, there is depression of the worst kind. Masses of humanity are beaten down and feel terrible about themselves. The world's inhabitants are loaded down with burdens, cares, concerns, worries, and fears.

Even in America and in church, what do you see? Quiet, sad, stone-faced, depressed people. Good people? Yes! Christian people? Yes! Valuable people to God? Yes! But people carrying a burden of depression. People who do not feel good about themselves or good about life.

**Trust in the Lord with all thine heart; and lean not unto thine own understanding.**

**In all thy ways acknowledge him, and he shall direct thy paths.**

**Be not wise in thine own eyes: fear the Lord, and depart from evil.**

**It shall be health to thy navel, and marrow to thy bones.**

> Honour the Lord with thy substance, and
> with the firstfruits of all thine increase:
>
> So shall thy barns be filled with plenty, and
> thy presses shall burst out with new wine.
>
> Proverbs 3:5-10

The first word in that section of verses is *trust*.
Even with all the present-day revelation of faith and
all the talk about releasing faith, standing on faith,
and believing God in faith, we do not hear very much
discussion of *trust*. A lack of trust in God is at the bottom of all our problems and difficulties. A lack of
trust is one of the major results of low self-esteem.
When you feel badly about yourself, you do not trust.
When you cannot trust God, you feel badly about
yourself. So you get into a cycle of doubting and not
trusting.

## Lack of Trust Began With Adam and Eve

The problems we have today and the answers
to them are all shown in the first few chapters of
Genesis. The problems Adam and Eve had are the
same problems we have in different settings and different cultures. God started man out on the right
track, but mankind got messed up fast.

> And the Lord God took the man, and put
> him into the garden of Eden to dress it and to keep
> it.
>
> And the Lord God commanded the man,
> saying, Of every tree of the garden thou mayest
> freely eat:
>
> But of the tree of the knowledge of good
> and evil, thou shalt not eat of it: for in the day that
> thou eatest thereof thou shalt surely die.
>
> Genesis 2:15-17

God placed the first man and woman in the garden that was east of Eden. That garden was full of everything they could possibly need or want. The garden was beautiful, comfortable, challenging, and abundant. They had work, and they had pleasure. They had responsibility, and they had enjoyment. Everything was there. God told Adam only one thing *not* to do. He said not to eat of the tree of knowledge of good and evil.

Man had a choice: to walk with God in His way or to make a left turn and walk in his own (which was really Satan's) way. Why did God put that tree in the garden in the first place? Because He did not want robots for children. He wanted people who wanted to walk with Him and fellowship with Him and who would do things His way because they loved Him. He wanted companions, not puppets on a string or robots programmed to a certain way. If man had no choice, no free will, he would be no more than a robot.

The choice was before that first couple. They could stay with God or walk away from God.

> Now the serpent was more subtil than any beast of the field which the Lord God had made. And he said unto the woman, Yea, hath God said, Ye shall not eat of every tree of the garden?
>
> And the woman said unto the serpent, We may eat of the fruit of the trees of the garden:
>
> But of the fruit of the tree which is in the midst of the garden, God hath said, Ye shall not eat of it, neither shall ye touch it, lest ye die.
>
> And the serpent said unto the woman, Ye shall not surely die:

> For God doth know that in the day ye eat thereof, then your eyes shall be opened, and ye shall be as gods, knowing good and evil.
>
> And when the woman saw that the tree was good for food, and that it was pleasant to the eyes, and a tree to be desired to make one wise, she took of the fruit thereof, and did eat, and gave also unto her husband with her; and he did eat.
>
> **Genesis 3:1-6**

Notice Adam and Eve were *together*. The Word says that her husband was with her. Most people have some religious idea that Adam was over on the other side of the garden naming caterpillars and rhinos while the devil sneaked up to Eve. They think Adam did not know what was going on, that Eve ate of the fruit and then came and told her husband.

They think Adam said, "I guess I might as well eat it also. If you are going to get kicked out of the garden, I don't want to be by myself."

*That is not what the Bible says.* That is religious tradition which puts the responsibility totally on the woman and excuses Adam because he loved her and did not want her to leave him. The Bible says they were both together, and they ate of the forbidden fruit together.

Adam knew what the devil was saying. He was listening to the devil. Although Satan was speaking to the woman, Adam knew what was going on because he was *with her*. Together they made a choice that caused all of their descendants to be born into sin and to live under sinful conditions. Why did they do that? Why did they eat of the fruit from the forbidden tree? Why did they listen to the devil? And after they listened, why did they not do what God said instead of what the devil said?

God said, "Do not eat of this one tree, and you will be blessed. I will take care of you. But eat of it, and you will die."

The devil said, "God just does not want you to have the best. He knows you will become like Him if you eat of it. You are going to be smarter and have more than you now have. You will get some good benefits if you do as I say."

Now the devil was not telling them to pattern their lives on God's ways and His Word in order to be like Him in character. He was telling Adam and Eve they could be *as* God, not like Him. He was tempting them with His own sin, an attempt to usurp God's place. Being children of God and like Him in all our ways is what the Father wants for us. Setting out to be as powerful *as* God, not just patterned in His image, is presumption and pride — the first recorded sin, Satan's sin that led to his downfall. That exaltation of self, or mankind, over God will always lead to a downfall. That concept is the very heart of humanism.

The reason they sinned is that *they did not trust God.* They did not trust Him to give them everything they needed. They did not trust in what He said, therefore they lost everything He had provided for them. *They did not trust the Word of God.* When Adam and Eve sinned, they lost their blessings, their peace, and their relationship with the Father. Most of the problems Christians have today come because they also do not trust the *Word* of God.

## Trust: One of Jesus' Main Concerns

When Jesus was on Earth, what did He spend much of His time trying to get people to do? He used many different kinds of examples and many words, but if you look at His overall message, it was *trust in the Father:*

"Believe in the Lord thy God," "Fear not," "Trust in the Lord," "All things are possible, *if you will only believe.*"

He tried constantly to get His people to believe the Old Testament. He said Heaven and Earth will pass away, but the Word of God will never fail. What do all His words add up to? *Trust God.* He tried to tell them that God was taking care of the birds. Were they not better than birds to God?

> **Therefore I say unto you, Take no thought for your life, what ye shall eat, or what ye shall drink; nor yet for your body, what ye shall put on. Is not the life more than meat, and the body than raiment?**
>
> **Behold the fowls of the air: for they sow not, neither do they reap, nor gather into barns; yet your heavenly Father feedeth them. Are ye not much better than they?**
>
> **Which of you by taking thought can add one cubit unto his stature?**
>
> **And why take ye thought for raiment? Consider the lilies of the field, how they grow; they toil not, neither do they spin:**
>
> **And yet I say unto you, That even Solomon in all his glory was not arrayed like one of these.**
>
> **Wherefore, if God so clothe the grass of the field, which to day is, and to morrow is cast into**

the oven, shall he not much more clothe you, O ye
of little faith?

Matthew 6:25-30

Jesus was saying, "Are you not worth more
than the flowers, the bushes, the plants, and the
trees? Are you not more valuable than they are? They
pass away, but you are going to live forever. Do you
not know that the Father will meet your needs, if you
trust Him?"

There are people today who think the Lord does
not want us to dress nicely, that He wants His people
to look poor and downtrodden and humble. God has
dressed this planet so beautifully that men have
stood in awe for thousands of years at the color and
beauty and glory of His creation.

And Jesus said, "Are you not better than
weeds? Are you not better to God than bushes? Are
you not worth more to Him than trees?"

We have looked at ourselves as being so unworthy in many situations. Jesus went on to state
specifically the things important to a believer.

> Therefore take no thought, saying, What
> shall we eat? or, What shall we drink? or,
> Wherewithal shall we be clothed?
>
> (For after all these things do the Gentiles
> seek:) (*Gentiles* really means "those without God or
> those who do not know God." Today we would say,
> "For after all, these are the things that sinners seek
> after.") for your heavenly Father knoweth that ye
> have need of all these things.
>
> But seek ye first the kingdom of God, and
> his righteousness; and all these things shall be
> added unto you.

149

**Take therefore no thought for the morrow:
for the morrow shall take thought for the things of
itself. Sufficient unto the day is the evil thereof.**
**Matthew 6:31-34**

Jesus said we will have enough to worry about tomorrow, so do not try to pile tomorrow's worries on today. Wait until tomorrow comes and then take care of it.

His message was, "Do not worry about life. Take no anxious thought, do not get 'uptight,' do not get nervous. Trust God."

Yet what are the major symptoms of sickness in people today? Heart attacks, ulcers, headaches, stomach aches, physical and mental breakdowns. Why? Many times the cause is diagnosed as "stress." What is stress? Worry, fear, taking anxious thought, anxiety attacks, concern for tomorrow. *No trust.*

Examine yourself, and you probably will find a lack of trust in God's desire or ability to take care of you permeating your thought life in many areas. Why do we not step out on some of the things the Bible says and act as if they are true (which they are)? Because we really do not trust that they are true. *Trust* is passive.

If a friend came along when I was having trouble walking and said, "Lean on me, and I will help you," I would be passive. I would have to trust him to hold me up, for he would be doing the work.

Leaning on the Lord, and relying on Him is not a burden! That is not work. Yet some people get all the faith tapes and books and work and struggle to get some faith. They get all worn out trying to use faith. All they need to do is *trust* the Lord. That is real faith. *Trust* is not difficult. *Trust* is letting Him carry the load.

> Come unto me, all ye that labour and are heavy laden, and I will give you rest.
>
> Take my yoke upon you, and learn of me; for I am meek and lowly in heart: and ye shall find rest unto your souls.
>
> For my yoke is easy, and my burden is light.
> Matthew 11:28-30

Religious tradition says, "Come unto me all ye that labor and are heavy laden, and I am going to give you some extra laws, some more do's and don't's. You are really going to get yourself a burden from the Lord."

The world says, "Come unto me, and I will give you fear and worry and trepidation. I will give you a newspaper and special news reports all day long so that you can be scared to death."

But Jesus still says, "Come unto me, and I will give you rest. You can trust me. You can lean on me. You can rely on me. I will carry you. I will lift you up with wings like an eagle's, and you can rest in me. I will take care of your needs."

We must trust Him, or we will never enjoy the rest that is available in Him.

A lack of trust results in fear, hatred, violence, lies, and depression. If I cannot trust God, I cannot trust my fellow man. When I cannot trust him, I become afraid of him. When I become afraid of him, I begin to hate him. Then I lie to him, and commit violence against him, and I begin to feel depressed. All of that starts with a lack of trust in God.

## Come to God as a Little Child

Do you really trust that God loves you? Do you think He is going to leave you stranded somewhere? If you have symptoms of sickness on your body, do you trust the love that God has for you? Or do you think He wants you to die from cancer? Do you think your heavenly Father wants to let you suffer in sickness, disease, and poverty, or do you trust that He loves you and is going to take care of you? Do you trust God's love for you, or are you scared that something bad is going to happen? Women, do you trust God to look after your husbands, or are you afraid your husbands will die and leave you alone? Many women are gripped with that fear.

Someone will say, "But we spent more money than we had, and we are in debt. How can I expect God to help me when I was so foolish?"

You can expect His help because He loves you. He loved you even when you were being foolish. Repent, and run back to Him. He will not leave you out there on your own.

Jesus said that unless you become (as trusting) as a little child, you cannot enter into the Kingdom of God. What do little children do? They just trust. Children do not ask for the theological implications of trusting. They just trust.

As adults, we become so analytical and logical that sometimes we become stupid. Come as a little child. Trust the love that God has for you. Trust in the

Lord with all your heart, and lean not to your own understanding. In all of your ways, acknowledge Him, and He will bring it to pass. (Prov. 3:5,6.) Trust will free you from worry, reliance on works, and bondage of all kinds. When you trust in the love of God, you are free from all guilt and all condemnation. You become very bold as a Christian when you get in tune (unity) and in touch with the love of God. You cannot fear when you know God's love is working on your behalf. When you trust His love, you do not have to work for your salvation. You do not have to struggle to get God to help you. You are free from doubt and worry, and you know that God cares for you and is looking out for you. You know that God wants to bless you with abundance, and you stand fast in that liberty.

Some people think they will not prosper until they do enough works for the Lord. They either do not know the Word or do not believe the Word when it says that man's works will not bring either salvation or blessings. Salvation and the blessings of God come because He loves us, and we trust Him. Some people walk under guilt and condemnation all their lives because of past mistakes or past sins. Carrying that guilt and condemnation around will block God's blessings.

Jesus says, "Do not get tangled up in all that bondage. Stand fast in the liberty wherewith I have made you free. You did not earn it, and you do not deserve it. But I gave it to you, so enjoy it."

Another result of trying to earn the blessings of God is pride — "I have worked this hard, Lord. Now you owe me. If I worked hard enough, then I deserve this. I have earned it."

No! Jesus made us totally free. Jesus blessed us. God provides His abundance freely and in love. All I have to do is accept it, *not because of what I do or who I am*, but because of what Jesus did and of Who He is. We need to trust Him in that way. Many Christians are trying to get God to do something that He has already done. You do not have to beg God to save you. Jesus already did it. All you have to do is accept salvation. The same thing is true of healing, deliverance, and all God's blessings. *He has already provided those things.* All we have to do is accept them. There is no way we can earn them.

*All of the concepts being discussed in this book are not designed to get God to do something for you. They are ways in which you can overcome your negative programming and become able to receive that which He has already done.*

He is the One who makes us righteous. We cannot earn it. We do not deserve it. We cannot *make* ourselves worthy. However, He has already made us worthy. If you will trust Him, you can be free from guilt and condemnation. There is nothing wrong with being happy, free, and excited every day. There is nothing wrong with that. Many believe that you have to have "down" days, "blue" days, and a certain amount of unhappiness. But Romans 8:1 says there is **no condemnation to them which are in Christ Jesus.**

God told Jeremiah how He feels about His people.

**For I know the thoughts that I think toward**

**you, saith the Lord, thoughts of peace, and not of evil, to give you an expected end.**

**Jeremiah 29:11**

We must trust the love that God has for us.

**Beloved, let us love one another: for love is of God; and every one that loveth is born of God, and knoweth God.**

**He that loveth not knoweth not God; for God is love.**

**1 John 4:7,8**

When you seek the Lord in prayer and worship and sing to Him, what do you think He feels? Does He think, "Oh, no. They are always bugging me about something!" God does not say that. He does not get upset. He has thoughts of peace toward us. He loves us, and when you begin to trust that love, you will cease from all of your dead works and from all of your worry.

Trust in God, and you will have confidence in yourself. Get rid of worry, fear, and doubt, and you will have no problem with low self-esteem. If you can trust the fact that God loves you, then you will see that you are worth loving. Then your vision will be established on a firm foundation, and you can begin to fulfill God's plan for you. You can start to become the child that He wants you to be and sees that you can be.

**Casey Treat** is a pastor, teacher, author, television host, and musician.

He is best known for his uncompromising and straightforward teaching on renewing the mind. Under his teaching, thousands have begun to receive peace, health, and prosperity in their lives.

As a teenager, Casey was involved heavily with drugs. In 1974, at the age of 19, he entered a drug rehabilitation center. During his years there, Casey began to change. He was born again and learned about renewing his mind to the Word of God.

He realized that the fast lane in which he had been living was in reality the slow lane to self-destruction. Casey attended Bible school and graduated valedictorian of his class. He was ordained into the ministry by Dr. Frederick K.C. Price at Crenshaw Christian Center in Los Angeles, California.

In January, 1980, he and his wife, Wendy, started *Christian Faith Center* in Seattle, Washington, with a group of 30 people. Others quickly responded to the straightforward message that God's Word works. As of January, 1989, more than 5,000 persons attend weekly services. In addition, conventions and special seminars bring thousands to receive teaching from some of the nation's leading ministers.

Casey Treat also is the founder of *Christian Leadership Institute*, which trains men and women to minister in the areas where God has called them. An outreach of this ministry is the *Ministry Training Institute*. It consists of teams of men and women who travel to different areas of the world training pastors to teach the abundant life of Jesus.

Casey is an adjunct professor at Oral Roberts University in Tulsa, Oklahoma, and serves on the board of directors for Church Growth International, founded by Dr. Paul Yonggi Cho in Seoul, Korea. Pastor Treat is the Northwest regional director for the International Convention of Faith Ministers (ICFM), as well as being a co-founding trustee of Charismatic Bible Ministries.

As a television host, Casey has met with remarkable success. His program is on stations across the country. He has been a guest on many other programs, both religious and secular, and has been the subject of numerous newspaper articles.

Casey travels more than 100,000 miles per year, taking his message of renewing the mind across the country and throughout the world. *Casey Treat Ministries World Outreach* has gone into Canada, the Philippines, Israel, India, and Africa. People are hungry for the Good News of Jesus, and Casey is committed to reaching out to people in every way possible.

Books and teaching tapes by Casey Treat covering a variety of subjects are distributed worldwide. His books have received endorsements from well-known Christian leaders such as Ed Cole, Marilyn Hickey, Lester Sumrall, T. L. Osborn, Rosey Grier, Dr. Cho, and others.

Casey is the drummer for his musical group called *Fire 'N Light*. This group includes powerful, anointed musicians, who are a testimony to God's plan for praise, worship, and music.

The Bible said in Romans 12:2: **Be not conformed to this world: but be ye transformed by the renewing of your mind that ye may prove what is that good, and acceptable, and perfect, will of God.** Because of Casey's teaching in this area, people are learning that through faith and through the renewal of the mind to God's Word, they can reap the benefits of the joyful, prosperous, and healthy life God wants them to have.

For a complete catalog of books and tape series
by Casey Treat, write to:

Casey Treat
P. O. Box 98800
Seattle, WA 98198

*Please include your prayer requests
and comments when you write.*

OTHER BOOKS BY CASEY TREAT

*God's Financial Program*

*Living the New Life*

*How To Receive the Baptism With the Holy Spirit*

*Positive Childbirth: God's Plan*

*Renewing the Mind: The Arena for Success*

*Your Vision Is Your Future*

*The Power Is in You*

*You Can Have a Prosperous Soul*

*You Make the Difference*

*Fulfilling God's Plan for Your Life*

*Living the Transformed Life*

Available from your local bookstore
or by writing:

**HARRISON HOUSE**
P. O. Box 35035
Tulsa, OK 74153